T

A Bicyc

SEAN BENESH

Urban Loft Publishers :: Portland, Oregon

The Bikeable Church
A Bicyclist's Guide to Church Planting

Urban Loft Publishers
2034 NE 40th Avenue #414
Portland, OR 97212
www.theurbanloft.org

Urban Loft publishes through CreateSpace (Amazon)

CreateSpace
7290 B. Investment Drive
Charleston, SC 29418
www.createspace.com

ISBN: 978-1479121533

Made in the U.S.A.

To the pedal-powered missiologists out there ...

Contents

About the Metrospiritual Book Series   5
Foreword by Caleb Crider   7
What Others Are Saying   9
Preface   13
Acknowledgements   16
Introduction   17

1 Journey Into Singlespeed Biking   21
2 Submerging Into Portlandia   28
3 How We Get Around Matters   36
4 Commuting Patterns and Churches   48
5 The Intersection of Missiology and
        Transportation Design   57
6 Why Grown Men Shave Their Legs   65
7 Reengagement   73
8 The DIY Bikeable Church   78
9 Simplicity   91

Appendix   101
Bibliography   103
Other Books by Urban Loft Publishers   105
About the Author   107
About Urban Loft Publishers   108

About the Metrospiritual Book Series

In my first book, *Metrospiritual*, I was looking for a term or a way to define what an urban-centric approach to faith and Scripture looks like. This came about as I wrestled through how do we reconcile the urban trajectory of humanity throughout Scripture, the current state of rapid urbanization and globalization, along with where we'll spend eternity. Similarly, with the church still viewing life, faith and Scripture either through a rural or a suburban lens, I believe it is time for a new set of lenses. This is what I call *metrospiritual*. I define it as, "taking an urban lens to the reading, understanding, interpretation, and application of Scripture." The *Metrospiritual Book Series* explores various aspects, elements, ideas, and methodologies, and the theology of what an urban-centric faith looks like as expressed in the city. A *metrospirituality* can have a shaping effect on the way the church lives in, loves, serves, embraces, and engages the city with the Good News of the Kingdom of God.

- Sean Benesh

METROSPIRITUAL BOOK SERIES

Other books in the *Metrospiritual Books Series*

The Multi-Nucleated Church: Towards a Theoretical Framework for Church Planting in High-Density Cities (2012) by Sean Benesh.

Foreword

Caleb Crider

For the most part, Sean follows the traffic rules as he rides his singlespeed road bike through the grid of urban Portland streets. I know this because I too live in Portland, Oregon, and I see my friend Sean all over town. Instead of driving a car or taking the bus, he rides nearly everywhere he goes.

Portland, of course, is a great place to be a bicyclist. It's the perfect fit for an experienced urban missiologist and church planter like Sean. In this city of creative young idealists, Sean's ideas about planting bikeable churches just seems to make sense. But don't replace your church's parking lot with bike racks just yet.

On the surface, *The Bikeable Church* is a book about making church more bike-friendly. But it's really much more than that. What's written here is a deeply missiological exploration of what it might look like to plant a church that takes a city's transportation systems into serious consideration. This is *contextualization*.

Sean's experience of moving to Portland and buying his bicycle are classic examples of joining a culture in order to point people to Christ. This is *incarnational ministry*, and it is a regular part of his life-rhythm.

It makes sense, then, that Sean would wonder about the results of our discipleship and church planting efforts. Forget importing models and methodologies from other places; the goal of the missionary is to plant churches that reflect the soil in which they're planted. This is *indigeneity*.

Sean isn't your typical "church planter," and this is not your typical church planting book. He doesn't start with a model, a sponsor, or a four-year plan. Instead, he tells the story of how he deliberately joined a social tribe in order to take the unchanging gospel of Jesus Christ to those who do not yet know him. It's great to read, but I have the privilege of seeing it first-hand. Sean practices what he preaches in *The Bikeable Church*.

Reading this book will make you want to rearrange your church's parking lot to make room for bikes. In the end, you may just do so. You may not. *The Bikeable Church* isn't just a book about bicycles, it's about thinking and acting like a missionary wherever God has you.

-- Caleb Crider
Co-founder, The Upstream Collective
www.theupstreamcollective.org

What Others Are Saying

"Sean has tapped into not only the heart of the missional movement but the ethos of his city for his call to be a 'bikeable' church. His message is built upon his experience as a cyclist and church planter, and his challenge follows the trend of urban centers around the world. Sean provides not only social observation and his own insights, but he gives practical ways to make your church bike-friendly and accessible to the two-wheeled vehicles and riders who are multiplying in your community. As a cyclist who lives in a suburb, I envy his culture of cycling and the opportunities he has to be the church in Portland, Oregon."

-- C. Gene Wilkes, PhD, is the author of *Jesus on Leadership* and *Evangelism Where You Live*. Gene is also Senior Pastor of Legacy Church, Plano, TX, and an avid cyclist.

"We live near Freiburg, Germany. A few days ago I had the chance to read *The Bikeable Church.* We have recently been part of a church planting team for a church in that city. As I read the book it brought back memories of our first public worship gathering and how many people on bikes showed up. I am very glad we had bike racks. We just did not have enough of them. This book addresses some very practical questions about starting churches in urban areas. Not only does it address some important missiological areas in urban church planting, but it also helped me think through the gathering location of our church plant and how many people will walk to church, bike to church, or take the tram to church."

-- Larry McCrary is the director of the Upstream Collective
www.theupstreamcollective.org

"Bicycles are a growing feature of many urban transportation landscapes. But how might the church relate to the bicycle lifestyle and mindset? In *The Bikeable Church,* Sean Benesh applies his missiological instincts and insights to answering this question in ways that only a bike enthusiast can!"

-- Craig Ott, PhD, Trinity Evangelical Divinity School, co-author of *Global Church Planting.*

"To be missional is to be culturally aware. To be missional is to be a strategic thinker. To be missional is to see social diversity. To be missional is to be alert to socio-cultural shifts. To be missional is to live into the mission of God. To be missional is to be "His ambassadors" of reconciliation and restoration of humanity with God. To be missional is to live "Christ" in contemporary time-context. To be missional is to look the mission of Christ through fresh eyes at the cultural shifts. Sean Benesh gets it! *The Bikeable Church* is more than a primer on church planting to a particular demographic. In clear, concise terms Sean communicates what it means to be a missional theologian. This is an insightful read igniting missional wisdom for our time and context."

-- Roger Trautmann, Associate Professor of Pastoral Ministry, Director of Mentored Ministry Formation, Multnomah Biblical Seminary/ Multnomah University, Portland, Oregon

"Sean's passion for cycling and church planting converge in this simple but enjoyable read. He does a good job as a missiologist unpacking insights for his readers. This book has created lots of good questions for me. As a cyclist and church planter strategist, I look forward to engaging my team with Sean's book."

-- Charles Campbell, Director of Church Planting, Southern Illinois Region

"Since Sunday at 10:00 am might be the most auto-centric time in America, *The Bikeable Church* presents an ecclesial vision that could only be imagined in Portland. Benesh reflects on his immersion in Portlandia's bike culture with the eye of a missiologist and urban planner. Although many U.S. cities are less bikeable, Benesh's call for churches to give attention to the intersection of transportation infrastructure, proximity, and culture is timely and transferrable across North America's urban landscape."

-- Scott Hagley, Ph.D., Director of Education, Forge Canada

"In his latest book Sean shares his insights on how living in a bikeable city enables people to rediscover the 'joy of slowness' – when we live closer to people and places, we have more time to simplify, slow down and relate with others. Increasingly, cities are realizing the 'car-centric' model cannot be sustained in the face of rising fuel prices, diminishing oil supply, rising congestion levels and declining public revenue. In Portland, bicycle-friendly policies have been a response to surging bike traffic. People are voting with their pedals. Similarly, churches must be responsive to cultural trends. Sean's book offers practical advice for churches seeking to be relevant in communities experiencing rapid-growth in bicycle use."

-- Denver Igarta, Transportation Planner, City of Portland Bureau of Transportation

"This is critically important book for anyone interested in a missional approach to urban ministry. What makes Sean Benesh's work so compelling is that he reflects and writes from the vantage point of a practitioner who through the thick descriptions of his own personal experiences stresses the need for immersing oneself in the culture we are trying to reach. Yet his work is not undergirded solely by the ethereal or anecdotal; he has done the grunt work of solid research as well. Sean masterfully challenges us to consider the fact that not only is the way we travel within the city an ecological concern, it has profound missiological implications as well. His intention is not to launch a personal vendetta against the automobile, but to present a well-thought out alternative for the way we plant churches in cities, recognizing that not everyone lives in a city that is bike-friendly. But in so doing he demonstrates that the choices we make with respect to our mode of transportation within the city matter for the simple reason that ... it even causes us to re-evaluate our roles as followers of Jesus in the city.

Sean effectively brings the whole concept of a *Bikeable Church* out of the hypothetical realm onto the terra firma of 'how to do it' through a generous list of practical and very do-able suggestions that virtually any church in almost any location could deploy. This personal, challenging and insightful work serves to benefit any who are concerned with reaching our cities with the Good News of Christ."

-- William (Bill) R. McAlpine, PhD, author of *Sacred Space for the Missional Church: Engaging Culture through the Built Environment*, and Professor of Practical Theology, Ambrose University College, Calgary, AB, Canada.

Preface

I wrote *The Bikeable Church* as a missiological exploration into church planting with the bicycle in mind. I live in Portland, Oregon, a city defined in many ways by the bicycle. Not only that, but Portland has become a brand that is synonymous with high-quality artisan bicycle craftsmanship and innovation. So much of the city is bicycle-oriented–from coffee to breweries to delivery services to a viable and legit mode of transportation. There is a reason why Portland was the first major American city to achieve the status of Platinum-Level Bike-Friendly City: It pushes the envelope in urban and transportation planning with the bicycle being a key component.

In his insightful and articulate book, *Pedaling Revolution: How Cyclists Are Changing American Cities,* Jeff Mapes, a local political reporter for *The Oregonian*, asks, "Can Americans really be seduced out of their cars in large numbers, at least for short trips?"[1] More and more we're seeing that here in Portland, people can indeed be seduced out

---

[1] Mapes, *Pedaling Revolution*, 10.

of their cars. But what about the church? To me, this is a conversation taking place on many levels and in many places throughout our cities and culture, and yet it seems like the church has refused to even come to the table. Maybe, possibly, the church doesn't know that this particular table even exists ...

My perspective for writing *The Bikeable Church* is from the vantage point of being a missiologist and a missionary to my own culture and city. In doing so, my attempt is to apply missiological principles and observations to my own city, add water, shake vigorously, and see what happens. We can easily apply these lenses when we look *over there*, but I am simply and humbly asking you to don those lenses for *here*. If there's to be a surge of bike-oriented, bike-friendly, and bikeable churches in America then Portland is the logical starting place.

My purpose for *The Bikeable Church* is to spin (no pun intended) forward the conversation around planting bikeable, bike-friendly, and bike-oriented churches, and to encourage existing churches to consider adjusting their ways to this burgeoning mode of transportation. As politicians, planners, engineers, architects, and professors push towards creating sustainable cities, one of the issues that comes to the surface is the need for healthier, greener, and cheaper modes of transportation. Enter the bicycle. While Portland has a robust scene of v-neck-wearing tattooed urban hipsters zipping by helmet-less on their singlespeed fixies, there are even larger numbers of bike commuters slogging through the rain into the downtown or children riding bikes to school. Can we conceive of church through the lens, grid, or framework of the bicycle? It's admittedly an odd question which I'm sure most (or no one) has really asked or contemplated before. Enter *The Bikeable Church*.

As with the first book in the *Metrospiritual Book Series*, my intention is to keep *The Bikeable Church* short, concise, and readable as far as length. These are what I call "bathroom books." Besides, since I'm targeting both church planters and bicyclists it means their time is limited. I don't want anyone to miss out on an epic bike ride or a coffee get-together with someone because they are slogging through page 513 in a tome about the minutia of church planting and bicycling.

Acknowledgements

I know this may sound corny, but I'd like to thank Portland for being Portland. Cities oftentimes are our greatest teachers ... if we'd only listen. I have learned much about missiology and church planting since moving to Portland. Not by immersing myself in more books, but instead by simply riding my bike and observing. From the bike messengers who hang out at Stumptown Coffee in Old Town, to the myriad of bicycle commuters hammering on their pedals through the rain, to the artisan bike-frame builders and bike mechanics I run into regularly at my coffee shop hang-out spot, I've learned much from watching them. Portland, you have taught me lots about what a pedal-powered church can look like where the primary mode of transportation is indeed the bicycle.

I'm always indebted to Frank Stirk, wonderful friend and great editor. It is always a privilege to work on projects with him.

Introduction

Excerpt from my blog The Urban Loft (www.theurbanloft.org)
May 21, 2012 | Portland, Oregon | "The Bikeable Church"

Over the weekend I stumbled onto a bikeable church. There was a church meeting literally across the street from where I live and I had no idea it was even there. I'll retell the story as I'm intrigued and inspired. I'm still processing this experience and maybe you can help me too ...

I walked across the parking lot and turned right at the corner of the building. Immediately in front of me was an assortment of bikes sitting out front of a nondescript building. The bikes were typical of Portland, mostly singlespeeds or other urban commuter bikes with fenders and lights rounding out the essentials. As I approached the opening of the building, the double doors were wide open and I could hear music and loud conversation emanating from inside. As I peered in, I saw a scene of about twenty to thirty cyclists all sitting and standing around chatting and laughing. There were just as many bikes inside as outside.

There was a place for refreshments and a large great table that could seat around twenty people. Add to that a variety of

17

other seats and benches, and this place could hold a good fifty people. Most people grabbed a drink and sat down to catch up with friends as well as meet new ones. Off to my right was a stage that was cool because it dropped down like a draw bridge. There was a projector overhead that was piping in the latest race taking place ... the *Tour de California*. Add to that the surround sound, dim lights, Portland's funky vibe, and it was quite a cool place for a church to gather.

I walked in and immediately the lead dude came up and chatted with me for a good fifteen minutes. We talked all-things mountain biking, bike-commuting in Portland, the race on the screen, and his dream for this space and gathering. He was super-friendly, but low-key. He is a veteran, having done this for many years, so there was no sense of hype or flash. Just a smile, a handshake, a greeting, and his time. Unbelievable.

I had learned that the staff of this group strategically moved within a radius of this building so that they all have only a five-, ten-, fifteen-minute bike commute in. Strategic.

I confess that I stood there with my son Camden at my side simply watching people. I made eye-contact with a number of people who smiled, nodded, and greeted me. There was this instant connection and community, even though I was a newbie as I had just walked in. My shaved legs and bike tire tattoo were a fit.

But ... it wasn't a church. It was a bike shop. This was simply a night where people gathered to watch a race together.

No Jesus, no Bible ... just a local bike shop showing a race on their big screen. I didn't mean to deceive you, but church, Jesus, and the Bible were probably the farthest things from anyone's minds.

Now mind you, one could loosely use the term "church" to define this gathering, as we know that the word "church" wasn't initially a spiritual term. More or less historically (1st century AD and before) "church" referred to the gathered assembly of a city. It was a group of citizens gathered for a specific purpose, most often for political reasons. This "assembly" that I had stumbled upon had most of the characteristics of what we think of as church minus the spiritual component of worshipping the Triune God. For me, it was a great missiological lesson.

When this bike shop moved into my neighborhood, I gladly welcomed its owner and workers and told them how stoked I was they were there. You see, their vision is much larger than simply a bike shop that sells and fixes bikes; it is in fact all about creating a community gathering place where all are welcome. Quite often they have events like this where they'll pipe in some bike race on satellite television, watch funny old movies like *Rad!*, and invite anyone and everyone. A bike shop with a massive screen, surround sound, a stage for concerts, and a bar. People meandered in, grabbed a locally crafted brew, sat down, and connected with one another. I saw singles, couples, and even families. Also, they're open until 10:00 EVERY NIGHT! When was the last time you heard of a bike shop that does that? Once they start rolling out more concerts they'll be open until midnight. I have truly found a home and a "fellowship."

If a bike shop can function like an "assembly," then why not the church? Why do we continue to insist on auto-based commuting patterns for church life and worship? What if we simply reduced the scale and scope to that which is bikeable and/or walkable? As missiologists one of the principles behind exegeting a city is to learn how people naturally gather for fellowship and community. Most often we still operate as a foreign import even within our own cities. It is time to think and act like urban missionaries.

Chapter 1

Journey Into Singlespeed Biking

Jerry was a mountain biking veteran. Having grown up in Tucson, Arizona he has been biking for decades. By the time I met Jerry he was a retired school teacher who began moonlighting as a hiking and mountain biking guide at the resort where I worked. But Jerry was a different kind of biker ... he didn't have shifters, derailleurs, or anything like that. Just a bike frame, handle bars, two wheels, front shocks, and brakes. Jerry was a singlespeed mountain biker.

It was my first experience with *one of those* kinds of bikers as they were certainly a different breed. Kind of like running into a former guitarist from an 80s hair band or a classic rocker, the singlespeed mountain bikers are (or at least were) a throw-back to yesteryear. More than the current fad for professional sports teams to wear throw-back jerseys, these bikers rode this way before it was even cool or desirable. To add to his legend, Jerry (like a classic rocker) would weave us tales of jumping on his mountain bike (before shocks) and riding to Globe on a mixture of trails and dusty desert washboard dirt roads. Globe is a hundred miles away. We sat around in awe. It was like listening to some bassist talk about playing with Jimi Hendrix.

Jerry's quirky personality matched his love for riding mountain bikes in a way we could deem "quirky." Come on, no gears? What about long technical climbs? Wouldn't you spin out when you're bombing down a singletrack trail? Like an impassioned evangelist, Jerry would do his best to convert us over to his kind of riding and biking lifestyle. I don't remember the conversation in crisp detail but I recall standing around in our bike shop talking with Jerry, as he wore me down about riding singlespeed. His go-to line was, "Sean, if you're going to do it, you have to be all-in. You have to give yourself six months minimum before you even think of riding a geared bike." It was like a Gospel presentation and I walked the aisle and converted on the spot.

I didn't get on my knees and pray a prayer; nor was there much fanfare, emotion, or applause. I just accepted Jerry's challenge to ride a singlespeed. The problem was I didn't have a singlespeed frame or a converter kit. No worries, because Jerry did. A short time later I met up with Jerry at his house where he rummaged through his garage that more resembled a mix between a bike shop, bicycle graveyard, and spare parts emporium. Alas, Jerry found his most prized frame for me. It was a chromoly KHS soft-tail that was surprisingly feathery light and already had a chain tensioner on it. He already had a converted real wheel set up with a singlespeed cog. No more excuses for me, I guess.

I paid Jerry a minimal amount for the frame, tire, and a Thomson seatpost. I brought my new chromoly steed home to my own bike shop garage and tossed it up on my bike repair stand. With a flurry I stripped my existing mountain bike of all the essentials I needed to build up this new bike. I ordered new front shocks, picked up a new stem, handle bars, and so forth and I was ready to roll. It was a quirky hodgepodge of a mountain bike with parts from three to four different bikes. The colors didn't quite match, but it didn't matter for I was a new singlespeed convert and was eager to "test my new faith."

That fateful day came on a trip up to Sedona. The allure of the mystical red rocks seemed like a perfect setting for my maiden voyage on my new, but old, gearless mountain bike. Within minutes I was huffing and puffing because all of a sudden I was standing up and hammering on the pedals rather than easily shifting into a gear that made pedaling uphill a breeze. At first I dismissed it as being due to the elevation. But as time went on I knew I was in trouble. You see, riding a singlespeed requires a completely different approach to mountain biking.

After an hour or so of riding, I was frustrated. I hated it. I had been promised temporal bliss in my newfound faith, but it was quickly turning into a nightmare. I just went through all of this effort, plus buying new parts, and now I had a bike that I detested and wanted to simply push off a cliff. Then I remembered Jerry's Yoda-like words: "If you're going to do it, you have to be all-in. You have to give yourself six months minimum before you even think of riding a geared bike." Drat, he was right. I knew I had to give myself a good six full months and there was no turning back on my conversion. I wanted the seeds of this fledgling faith to find good soil, germinate, and grow. If you've ever made the switch from a PC to a Mac, you'll understand a little of the feeling. You're promised eternal (and temporal) bliss by switching to the ever-so-trendy Mac, but after the first day you find yourself deeply frustrated. Nothing is the same and you have to completely reorient yourself to not only a new computer, but a new way of interacting with a computer. But once familiarity sets in, you're set for life. The same happened with me and my singlespeed.

On the southeast side of Tucson is a great little network of trails called Fantasy Island. While there were no Mr. Roarke's, Tattoo's, or flowery leis being placed around your neck, it is surprisingly a fun series of singletrack cross-country mountain bike trails designed specifically for mountain bikers. It is like Disneyland for mountain bikers. I had ridden there many times with my previously geared bike. I even had it down to a science of about exactly how long it'd take me to ride a loop which I tried to better each ride. I had hit a wall with my times and plateaued. But when I rode my singlespeed bike for the first time at Fantasy Island I smashed my best time by fourteen minutes. I was shocked!

The thing with riding a singlespeed is it is all about momentum. This particular trail was a series of descents and short climbs, tight corners, and stretches of all-out sprinting. The trick at the top of a fast descent is to simply let it rip. No holding back. Why? Because on the climb back out, you can't simply shift into an easier gear and slowly pedal out. You bomb the hill and let your momentum begin carrying you up until you get to the point where you're out of the saddle hammering hard on the pedals just to make it out without putting your foot down. Whenever I approach hills, I speed up to build momentum, get up out of the saddle, and hammer up the hill as fast as I can. With a geared bike, it is always easy to simply drop into a granny gear and leisurely climb. Not so with singlespeeds.

That was then and this is now. It has been years since I've lived in Tucson and I'm no longer a mountain biking guide. I have plunged headlong into all things urban and now live in the inner city of Portland, Oregon. I vividly remember when we first moved to Portland because the NE neighborhood we live in is seemingly one long bike parade. I had heard of Portland's reputation as being bike-friendly, but I was not prepared for what I saw. I stood there by the front door and was mesmerized by all of the pedal-powered cyclists zipping around the neighborhood. You could immediately tell, based upon attire, that these were not weekender cyclists, but instead this was their primary mode of transportation. Businessmen in dress slacks, women in skirts, and a vast array of hipsters in skinny jeans and appropriately placed facial hair and exposed tattoos. What was most bewildering were all of the cyclists riding singlespeed urban commuter bikes. I was hooked. If Portland wasn't heaven, then at least it was a suburb of it.

Since taking the singlespeed baton from Jerry, I developed my own quirky approach to biking that resembles this way of riding. I steer clear of spandex and prefer building bikes from scratch rather than buying them complete in a shop. Naturally when we moved into Portland I knew I needed to join in the mass bike culture and most importantly on a singlespeed. I had found my people and was ready to participate in cruising the streets on a singlespeed, drinking lots of coffee, shopping in thrift stores, wearing funny hats, and listening to Mumford and Sons. I had wanted to simply go out and buy an urban singlespeed commuter bike but since the market was and is hot for them they were too much for me to drop $500 on. (I'm cheap.) I simply decided to get road slicks for my mountain bike, tweak the gear ratio, and I'd be set. Or so I thought.

One fateful day as I was perusing road slicks and such at a local bike shop, I wishfully walked past the section of bikes that were all singlespeeds. One in particular caught my attention. I stood there, looked at it, and Katie, my wife, came over to see what I was staring at. When she saw me, she said without hesitation, "Why don't you take it for a spin?" "Don't tempt me," I told her. I then flipped over the price tag and almost gasped ... it was dirt cheap. After I flagged down a bike shop employee he told me even better news ... the bike was another 40 percent cheaper than what the price tag displayed. Within minutes I was cruising the bike on the hills around the bike shop in downtown Portland. I was smitten, but I was still cheap.

Inevitably Katie wore me down and convinced me to buy the bike. What few components the bike had were bottom of the barrel and would eventually need to be replaced. But since I'm semi-handy with bikes it was no big deal. Over time I began swapping out parts as I found them on the cheap in the used parts bins at various bike shops or on super-sale. First the handle bars, then the grips, stem, front wheel, crank set, seatpost, and then back wheel. I added fenders since it rains most of the year in Portland, lights so I'd be seen. Throw in cuffed pant legs, a waterproof messenger bag and a bike lock, and I was "in the tribe." I was a singlespeed urban cyclist living in inner-city Portland. Epic.

Chapter 2

Submerging Into Portlandia

Portland is poser-resistant and poser-retardant. Meaning, it is the land of the cool, the hip, and the trendy. But the caveat is that while everyone aspires for higher levels of coolness you can't reveal that you are really trying. Brett McCracken quips, "To label oneself a 'hipster,' then, is either a fun exercise in irony or just a misguided platitude that exacerbates our increasing inability to understand languages, labels, and ourselves."[1] He later on writes, "Hipsters absolutely loathe the word *hipster.* And yet, ironically, the word is almost exclusively uttered by hipsters themselves."[2] Coolness and hipness need to be natural, second nature, and not forced. I had come from living in a predominantly Asian neighborhood in Vancouver, BC, where I did my best to fit in regarding wardrobe and hairstyle. Not that I'm a chameleon, but missiologically speaking, aren't we to always attempt to adopt the culture, habits, and lifestyle of the cities in which we find

[1] McCracken, *Hipster Christianity*, 21.

[2] Ibid., 51.

ourselves whether Vancouver, London, Paris, Amsterdam, or Tokyo? As the apostle Paul wrote, "To the weak I became weak, that I might win the weak. I have become all things to all people, that by all means I might save some. I do it all for the sake of the gospel, that I may share with them in its blessings."[3]

When I lived in Tucson I had intentionally adopted the lifestyle and fashion of a desert-dwelling Tucsonan. For most of the year it meant sparse clothing because of the heat. Not a loin cloth, mind you, but shorts, tees, and sandals. In Vancouver I attempted to dress at the confluence of urban-Asia-meets-western-Europe. Now that I'm in Portland? Well, back to the thrift stores. With that said, I don't think I could attempt to wear skinny jeans. I would be spotted a mile away and derided as a poser.

So I'm in Portland ... now what? I have a bike (check), bike-related tattoo (check), a passion and love for coffee (check), background and experience in the cycling world as a mountain biking guide (check), and yet I still have much to learn about the nuances of Portland's urban bike culture. For starters, "Portland residents use the bike for transportation more than any other large city in America, and the city has gained an international reputation for encouraging bicycling."[4] Panic ensued locally last year when for some odd reason

---

[3] 1 Corinthians 9:22-23.

[4] *Pedaling Revolution*, 142-143.

Portland was demoted to second place as being the most bike-friendly city in America. Not that there was ever a doubt for Portlanders that we're #1, but we have a reputation to uphold. The voting more or less went like this ... since Portland always wins, people simply got tired of voting Portland as #1 year after year. Anyone who's biked in Portland and America's other bike-friendly cities knows that there really is no comparison. Sorry Minneapolis, Boulder, Indianapolis, Davis ... it is not even close. So how do I submerge myself into Portland's bicycling culture?

That unassuming question really is quite detailed and complicated in terms of application. The bike scene in Portland is so deep, wide, and multi-faceted that there are multiple entry points and they don't always even overlap. Here's what I mean. You can approach the bicycle culture and conversation from the non-profit angle of community development (Community Cycling Center[5]), advocacy (Bicycle Transportation Alliance[6]), education (Transportation planning degree at Portland State University[7]), transportation planning and architecture (Alta Planning + Design[8]), bike

---

[5] http://www.communitycyclingcenter.org.

[6] http://btaoregon.org.

[7] http://www.pdx.edu/usp/node/37#transportation.

[8] http://www.altaplanning.com.

frame building (Sweatpea Bicycles[9]), bike shop culture (Velo Cult[10]), bike-related businesses (SoupCycle[11]), and that is only the tip of the iceberg! There's cyclocross (which is huge here), mountain biking, double-decker tall biker, unicycles, group bike rides to school, and so much more. My immediate question is this ... where is the church in this?

I made the conscious decision to jump headlong into the bike culture of Portland. As I just explained, it is in some ways more complicated than I initially realized. Which aspect of the bike scene am I going to immerse myself in? There's an enormous difference between raingear-clad middle-aged bike commuters with more bright neon colors than an 80s breakdancing movie (with an array of blinking lights that make a UFO seem boring) versus skinny jeans-wearing mid-20s hipsters riding fenderless fixies. Do I go the route of advocacy? Community development? Planning policy? Education? I think I've landed somewhere in the middle of it all.

Last fall I took a class at Portland State University (PSU) in urban studies. One of the draws for the program and the school is that Portland is an amazing living urban laboratory to tackle urban studies, urban planning, transportation, and community development. The first class I took was

---

[9] http://www.sweetpeabicycles.com.

[10] http://velocult.com.

[11] http://www.soupcycle.com.

specifically on urban economics and spatial structure. Most evenings I'd hop on my bike and ride to and through downtown to the university. PSU is unique in that the campus is urban and located in the heart of downtown Portland which means it is accessible via MAX light rail line, the modern streetcar, bicycle, on foot, and car. My bike ride through downtown was and is always mesmerizing. One quickly learns that the quickest way through the city is truly by bike. With ample bike lanes the traffic lights are even set according to the speed of the average cyclist which means you can easily get through sections of downtown without ever stopping. It is not all ideal as a recent downtown bike-related death revealed how vulnerable cyclists still are.[12]

Downtown Portland in many ways favors the cyclist. While everyone else is paying for parking, the cyclist simply locks his or her bike in the many bike staples or corrals. Each week I'd lock up my bike on campus with hundreds of other bikes. After class would find me zigging and zagging my way back through downtown at night on my bike with my lights annoyingly blinking to let motorists know that I am present. I found that navigating the downtown streets at night was not only doable but enjoyable. This is a far cry from the way Portland was only twenty years ago. As bicycling planning legend Mia Birk explained in 1993, "What was I thinking? That Portland was already like Amsterdam or Copenhagen?

---

[12] Maus, "Woman dies after collision with 18-wheeler on SW Madison."

Bicycling conditions are deplorable, scary. I wouldn't send my worst enemies onto these roads."[13]

Now? Not very many people who've biked in Portland would hesitate at our title of most bike-friendly city in America. In inner-city NE Portland I recently read an article that revealed fifteen percent of commuters commute via bike. It is the highest percentage in the city. While these are not Amsterdam numbers, it is still movement in the right direction. In many ways Portland is only at the beginning. "The bike network, combined with the city's transit system and planners' focus on developing amenities in neighborhoods, allows people to access work, shopping, and social and recreation destinations without a car. Portland's emerging reputation for a car-free lifestyle is a significant draw for a new creative class, especially bike-related artisans."[14]

Most mornings find me hopping on my chromoly singlespeed steed and heading over to the coffee shop. I have fallen in love with Ristretto Roasters on North Williams so I spend a good amount of time there. When we first arrived in Portland we lived a half a mile away and now I trek a good three miles for my cup of joe. It is worth it. Not only for the great locally roasted artisan coffee, but the place is a hub for inner North and Northeast Portland's cycling community. All

---

[13] Birk, *Joyride*, 6.

[14] Heying, *Brew to Bikes*, 110.

around Ristretto, local businesses cater to the bike culture. In the same building as Ristretto there are Sweetpea Bicycles that makes custom frames for women and Sugar Wheel Works[15] that focuses on custom wheelsets. Both Sweatpea and Sugar share space. Across the road is the Hopworks BikeBar[16] and next to that is the United Bicycle Institute[17] that offers bicycle mechanic classes and certification. As you can already surmise, this place is a hotbed for the bicycling culture.

When I'm at Ristretto I can't help but notice the clientele coming in and out during the course of the morning. I'm there roughly from 8:00 AM until about noon so I see a lot of people. I watch as some of the local brewers come in for coffee each morning before they venture back to their artisan hand-crafted beer brewing. At times I notice various bicycling-related employees walk in as they don their company's paraphernalia ... Shimano, Chris King, etc. Along with that is the constant stream of hipsters coming in, usually with their right pant leg rolled up, which is a clear indicator that they biked over to Ristretto.

As mentioned, Portland is one of the epicenters of the bike culture in the U.S. In fact, Portland has now become a brand in and of itself. "The explosion of bicycle builders in the city and media coverage of it has given 'made in Portland' a

---

[15] http://www.sugarwheelworks.com.

[16] http://hopworksbeer.com/general-info/bikebar.

[17] http://www.bikeschool.com.

new and strongly positive meaning that bicycle enthusiasts around the country increasingly recognize."[18] Portland is truly a unique place to be. It offers me the ideal backdrop in which to explore the confluence of bicycling and church planting.

One might assume that because of Portland's brand, reputation, and reality of being a bicycling mecca, with progressive urban and transportation policy, advocacy groups, and a multitude of businesses that cater to this burgeoning culture that the church would be right there in the conversation–and that especially church planters, pastors, and urban missionaries, in applying the latest missiological strategies, would be crafting and designing new ways of doing and being the church, including bicycle-focused church planting. Sadly, that is not true. For the most part, the church and church planting are still stuck in the 1980s love affair with the automobile. The culture of Portland is moving towards sustainable transportation while the church is seemingly happy with being car-oriented. Am I missing something?

---

[18] *Brew to Bikes*, 118.

Chapter 3

How We Get Around Matters

The life of the church has fallen in step with the larger cultural story of how we get around. "For 100 years, we have planned and designed our cities around personal automobile travel. We have cemented our auto addiction through our land-use practices, management of traffic, use of publicly funded space and layout of our buildings. We have gotten so used to driving everywhere for every trip that we have forgotten how to use our bodies to fulfill our basic transportation needs."[1]

On most fronts, this is normative, assumed, and missiologically speaking, right on. However, when it comes to cities like Portland bucking the trend, the church is lagging behind. "Too often in church planting it is easy to become negligent to the overall urbanism of one's host city as an overall influential factor as to how church is done and expressed."[2] One of the problems lies in political jockeying,

---

[1] Birk, *Joyride*, vi-vii.

[2] Benesh, *The Multi-Nucleated Church*, Chapter 1.

name-calling and labeling, and partisan loyalties. That is to say, if one's opposing political party advocates for safer streets, pedestrian- and bicycle-oriented transportation, and congestion fees, then regardless of how much one values those measures, they'll interpret these policies through a partisan political lens.

At this point in the book, I am at a crossroads. It is tempting to back up the dump truck of research and data in regards to transportation costs, planning and policy changes, changing economics and the resultant impact on the city's built environment, peak oil, global warming, and so forth. I could quote a lot of really smart professors, cite obscure academic journals *ad nauseum*, fill the bottom of each page with more footnotes than a dissertation, and we'll be well on our way to boredom (well, of course unless you enjoy those things ... like me). But my intention is to keep the tenor of this book light, playful, and simple. Besides, I ride a singlespeed which means I'm all for simplicity.

Let's step outside of academia and imagine a scene together. You're sitting at the bar at the Velo Cult bike shop on the Hollywood District in NE Portland (where I live ... in Hollywood, not at the bike shop). Wafting through the air is a mixture of smells–bike grease, rubber tires, new clothes on the racks, new bike gear in general, wood, and beer. In other words, you're fully present in the here-and-now rather than having your nose stuck in a book. On the other side of the bar is one of the bike shop employees and next to you is yet another employee. It is 9:00 PM on a weeknight. And while the bike shop is still open, the stream of customers has now mostly trickled away.

The conversation, as always, is about all-things-bikes and the bike culture in Portland in general. The Velo Cult crew are mostly recent transplants to Portland from San Diego. When asked why the transition, one of the employees simply admitted, "We realized that we were running a Portland bike shop in San Diego." The cultural climate here was and is much more conducive to what they are about, which is more than selling and fixing bikes. It is about getting immersed in the bike culture, providing a gathering space for the bike community, and promoting it as a viable way of life and transportation. You see, the bicycle is more than a recreational piece of exercise equipment. It is even more than a mode of transportation. It is a culture, a way of life, and even a mentality. Whether we realize it or not, our transportation (how we get around) actually defines us.

While sitting at the bar (in case you're wondering, I don't drink), the conversation turns towards bike transportation. Both guys live within a five- to ten-minute bike ride from work, and as far as I know do not even own cars. In Portland, who needs a car, anyway? If you really do need a car, there are always Zipcar[3] and the Car2Go[4] car-share programs. We don't

---

[3] http://www.zipcar.com.

[4] http://www.car2go.com.

realize how expensive it is to simply have a car. Earl Blumenauer noted, "A bike costs less than a dollar a day to maintain, annual operational costs for a car approach $8,000. For the cost of single lane of urban freeway, an entire city can be outfitted with safe and accessible bike connections."[5] Why not live a hassle-free life on a bike and when needed, rent a car for thirty minutes, an hour, a day, or a weekend? The cost savings alone on a yearly basis would be staggering.

We lived car-less in Vancouver, BC, for nearly two years, but now that we've moved to Portland, we do have an automobile again. And a gas-chugging V-8, at that. Because of Katie's health issues, most of the time she is not up to biking, so I'm grateful to have a vehicle. Plus we end up constantly transporting longboarders around the city and region to various skate spots and events which is another added bonus. Did I mention we have heated seats? Whoops, I'm not building my case on the evils of car-based transportation. Like most people, we're not purists, although they are here in large numbers. For me, though, my way of life revolves mostly around the bicycle. When I am running short on time and need to travel a good distance, I will hop on my scooter. Since it costs me about $2 every other week to put gas in it, I don't think too long and hard about using it from time to time. But I mostly enjoy bike travel because of the health benefits.

---

5 *Joyride*, iii.

Once in a while I'll need to buy a new part for my bike. Wear and tear from all of the road grime takes a toll on a bike in a wet climate like Portland. When I tell Katie that I need to get a new part she sometimes jokingly says to me, "Again?" I then remind her that we only have to fill up our SUV a few times to equal how much it'd cost for me to buy an entire new singlespeed bike. I tell her, "It's my MoDo" – mode of transportation. Soon afterwards, I'm swapping out bike parts and ready to hit the road.

Since I get around mostly on bike, I end up not venturing too overly far away from our hub and home in NE Portland. Sure, during the lunch hour, I daily ride for an hour to an hour and a half for exercise which means I travel some good distance, but I mostly stay in my part of the city ... inner NE, inner SE, North Portland, and downtown. I have still yet to even make it out to most of the suburbs. I also have the luxury of living in a higher density part of the city which affords me the opportunity to live this kind of lifestyle. "The denser a city the less its residents drive, the more they use transit, walk, and bike. This suggests the people drive mostly because they have no other alternative. Providing nearby density to support transit, walking, and bicycling is a critical component to lessening oil dependence and reducing greenhouse gas emissions."[6]

---

6 Newman et al, *Resilient Cities*, 84.

What do our transportation choices communicate? If the message is the medium, then what are we communicating – and to whom – with choices we make about how we get around?

In cities like Portland, there is an underlying value system placed upon modes of transportation. Fair or not, right or wrong, this is still a reality. Culturally the bike is at the top of the transportation food chain. Admittedly, this is a cultural preference for urban Portland and doesn't necessarily reflect the city's transportation policies since it budgets a lot more for maintaining roadways compared to making bike lanes. But the bike is a priority. While the majority of commuting is still by car, it does not diminish the mythical place of the bike in the eyes of urbanites.

Recently Kona Bikes came out with a video called *How Bikes Make Cities Cool - Portland.*[7] The video is described as "a five-minute mini documentary that explores the thriving bicycle culture resident to one of North America's most progressive metropolises. Filmed entirely by bike, with support from longtime Kona Portland dealer Sellwood Cycles and resident Team Kona athletes Erik Tonkin and Matthew Slaven, we spent the better part of a week talking to commuters, following kids to school and capturing the friendly vibe and funky nature of a city that embraces self-propelled commuting at the heart of its identity." In the video,

---

[7] http://vimeo.com/38385810.

which summarizes Portland well, a young woman who was commuting by bike over one of the bridges that spans the Willamette, says, "It's just accessible. You can show up to a party or a bar in heels and a short dress on a bike and nobody notices." How we get around does indeed matter. It also communicates much.

The beauty of the gathering of cyclists at the Velo Cult bike shop that I wrote about earlier reveals that there can actually be larger gatherings of people who gather primarily on a bike. I see it daily. I live on the fourth floor of an apartment building and right below me is a main bicycle thoroughfare. I see groups of cycling children commuting to school. There are scores of cyclists who cruise by on their way downtown or back the other way after work. Oftentimes, throughout the day and evening, I can be sitting in my living room or out on the patio, and below me I hear the sounds of cyclists. I hear people chatting away with one another, the familiar sound of the bike bell dinging, the sound of shifting gears, and the occasional "pop" sound when a chain skips during shifting.

I have my bike repair stand on our outside patio. When it isn't raining, I enjoy tossing my bike up on the stand to work on it. As I'm working on my bike, I notice and watch the vast array of cyclists pedaling around the neighborhood. It is a beautiful sight to behold with their colorful rainproof jackets and all kinds of bikes. I watch as well the numerous cross streets where cyclists are also merging onto the main bike route. Many times I stand there leaning against the railing where I can watch what is taking place at the Velo Cult bike shop across the road. At 10:00 PM in the evening, I see them turn off the lights in the shop and head home. More than simply a mode of transportation to get from Point A to Point B, the bicycle matters.

Given the focus of this book, I am purposely staying away from all the conversations about peak oil, the automobile manufacturing industry, Fordism/Post-Fordism, and all of that. I don't inwardly harbor any grand conspiracy theories about people who drive cars and don't bike. While I applaud people who live car-free and get around strictly on a bike or public transit, I also know it is not for everyone. Most American cities are simply not dense enough nor set up yet to foster a bicycle culture, but they should. Cities, or parts of most cities, that are truly more dense could and should indeed explore alternative modes of transportation. "Nonmotorized transport (NMT) – bikes and walking – need to be given priority over motorized vehicles, especially in dense centers."[8]

That said, there is a strong conviction that favoring and promoting alternative modes of transportation is truly a movement towards creating (or retrofitting) healthy and sustainable cities. "The bike offers a non-polluting, non-congesting, physically active form of transportation in a country and in a world, that increasingly seems to need such

---

8 *Resilient Cities*, 98.

options."[9] Not only that, but when personal cars are removed as the kingpin of the primary mode of transportation it makes for a more equitable city. "Ideas about compact and transport-based cities are ways in which cities could impact less upon climate change. Retrofitting existing car-based cities with public transport- and pedestrian-based movement systems would go a long way towards reducing fuel demands. It has also been suggested that cities planned in this way are more equitable in terms of providing good accessibility to both wealthier and poorer urban residents and overcoming spatial marginalization."[10] You see, how we get around actually *does* matter.

It matters because it communicates much about our value of a sustainable and equitable city. It matters because it even causes us to reevaluate our roles as followers of Jesus in the city. Is our model, "Screw the city because in the end times it'll be annihilated"? Or is it, "God desires to redeem our cities as we witness the larger story of the in-breaking of the Kingdom of God at hand"? Advocating for bike-friendly cities is not simply some neo-hippie Portland thing to do. Encouraging people to drive less and bike more (or use public transit) actually creates even more ripe conditions for the spread of the Gospel.

---

[9] Mapes, *Pedaling Revolution*, 13.

[10] UN-HABITAT, *Global Report on Human Settlement 2009*, 14.

An auto-based lifestyle is often associated with anonymity and loneliness. "There are many reasons – environmental, economic, health, and social – to overcome car dependence."[11] We've lost touch. We've lost touch with our bodies, with our cities, and with our neighbors. We're all living in our personal bubbles with their faceless rows of garages that encourage solitude. When you bike you're aware of your surroundings, you can talk en route, there is a lot of eye contact and nods to other riders, conversations happen at red lights and stop signs, there are fist bumps with strangers, and you get to know your city intimately and up close. As church planters or missionaries, what could be better than that?

Added to the current dilemma there is a growing trend of younger successive generations eschewing the auto in favor for alternative modes of transportation. Much of the reason is that the urbanization process is pulling young adults not only into cities, but into central cities *en masse.* Remember when you turned sixteen? I do. My Mom got me out of school so I could go to the DMV to take my driver's test. I barely passed (which should've been a warning for my early years of driving), but with smiles and newfound freedom I drove my land yacht (1982 Pontiac Grand Prix) back to school. I even cut the corner short pulling into the school driveway and popped up on the curb. Nevertheless I was free ... free to cut donuts on the icy school parking lot before morning basketball

---

[11] *Resilient Cities*, 87.

practice in the winter, to jump about forty feet (at least it felt like it) at "thrill hill" outside of town, and to get pulled over by the police LOTS of times in my first two years. But emerging generations are looking at the car and saying, "No thanks, I'll bike or I'll take transit."

Automakers are scratching their heads as to why younger adults are forgoing buying cars. "No matter how cool they make them, young people aren't taking the bait. It's a cliché, but it probably is true, that when young people graduate from college they tend to move to the big city. A car would only complicate their lives - instead of a car, they take a taxi, or they'll rent a car for a trip out of town. And this way, they don't have to pay exorbitant parking fees when the car is not needed."[12] *Motor Trend* also highlighted this challenge in an article entitled, "Why Young People Are Driving Less." Todd Lassa writes,

> Automakers pitch new small cars, from the Fiat 500 to the Ford Fiesta and Chevrolet Sonic to the Acura ILX, as models designed to appeal to America's urban-oriented Generation Y. Marketing experts fill product presentations with statistics and anecdotes of how tuned-in youth fetishize smartphones, the Internet, and keeping in touch with friends via Facebook from their loft apartments in "walkable" cities. Cars? Not so much. The problem begins with the assumption that youth moving back to the cities want A- or B-segment hatchbacks, when they're

---

[12] International Making Cities Livable, "Why Aren't Young People Buying Cars?"

more likely to spend the money on smartphones, tablets, laptops, and $2000-plus bikes.[13]

You see, how we get around matters. Does how we get to church matter and what is it communicating to younger generations when we're operating in "old" transportation paradigms? That lone question opens up a Pandora's Box of other related questions about the intersection between church planting, missiology, and bicycling. Trust me, that intersection exists.

---

[13] Lassa, "Why Young People Are Driving Less."

Chapter 4

Commuting Patterns and Churches

I started off the last chapter by asking, does how we get around matter? By now you'll have guessed that my answer is indeed "yes." So should it also matter how we get to church? Come on, that's a bit extreme, isn't it? Isn't it? How would women in pastel dresses and high heels on a rainy mid-February day in Portland make it? Or what about the girl in pigtails wearing that lovely wool sweater that grandma knitted? Or hey, what about the guy in the polyester suit? Did you know that polyester dries faster than cotton? How's he going to bike? What if he hits a puddle? What if the whole streetscape is like one large puddle in the rain? What to do?

Local Portland author, April Streeter, writes in her book, *Women on Bikes: A Handbook and How-To for City Cyclists,* about what it would take to get more people to bicycle, especially women. Fashion and safety considerations are top priorities. She writes, "It's pretty simple. Women go riding as soon as the roads feel safe."[1] And it's not just women; guys

---

[1] Streeter, *Women on Bikes*, 19.

too want to look good and feel comfortable when riding. "Biking is a form a freedom; in our modern, resource-constrained world we could use more of it. I sense a new era of cycling is upon us, when fashion designers appropriate bikes as their favorite prop and make 'bike-friendly attire' part of their collection."[2] So, yes, how we get around does indeed matter. But does it matter for the church?

I am certainly not the first person to ask questions around the topic of transportation options for how the church gathers. Does how we get to church matter? Does bicycling to a worship gathering mean anything? Recently a friend pointed me to a blog post on the U.S Catholic website. The article was called, "Have you ever ridden a bike to church?" The author, Meghan Murphy-Gill, writes, "Since we're a Catholic magazine, and I'm always looking for good Catholic stories, all this commuting by bike has had me thinking about how Catholics get to church. With the current trends of merging and supersizing parishes to accommodate both dwindling Mass attendance and the increasingly sprawling and less concentrated Catholic populations, I imagine for non-city dwellers, the seemingly only way to get to church is by car, which of course means bigger parking lots. And trying to get in and out of a parking lot before and after Mass can challenge even the most saintly among us."[3]

---

2 Ibid., 11.

3 Murphy-Gill, "Have you ever ridden a bike to church?"

I'm going to inch out onto a limb here. Ah heck, I'm shuffling out ... maybe skipping as I go. Here's my untested theory. Ready? My guess, hunch, hypothesis, hankering is that 97 to 98 percent of Christians in Portland gather for worship via their personal automobile. Now before you fire off a volley of emails to the publisher to complain, hear me out. I confess that for now ... so do I (gulp). Now mind you, that's not what we're building towards in our own church plant. But for now at the church we're currently plugged into, it is a reality. You can now click delete on that email. My intention in advocating for bikeable churches is not to make the auto evil, but to simply point to an alternative (and complementary) way of doing and being church.

While I didn't stand outside a hundred different churches with a clipboard counting cyclists on their way to worship, nor wear a white lab coat in the process, or don a fashionable hairnet (you know, for looks, of course), I did contact a number of pastors and church planters from various cities across the U.S. and Canada. I was simply asking them for a sampling of how bikeable are our current churches and new church plants. Mind you, the survey results will probably be a tad tainted because the vast majority of churches surveyed were urban churches. As a result, what is afforded to them is the density that urban contexts provide over lower-density suburban settings. With that said, surely, if American and Canadian urban churches are not bikeable, bike-friendly, nor bike-oriented, then the suburban churches don't stand a chance. Again, the built environment of the city does influence much.

I fired off an email to roughly thirty pastors and church planters who represented both established churches as well as new church plants. Here are the questions that I asked:

1. Name of your church? Location? (i.e. First Church, NE Portland)
2. How many people meet weekly at your church for the "main gathering?"
3. How many of that group commutes to your worship gathering via bicycles?
4. Does your church promote/encourage bicycle transportation to your gatherings/events/church life? How? (how are you promoting ... or not? Do you have bike parking?)
5. Anything else you want to add?

I have included the survey results in an Appendix at the back of the book, minus the names of the churches and the cities in which they're located. However, I do indicate whether they were urban or suburban.

What is interesting about the timing of the survey, as well as this book in general, is that *Bicycling* magazine just released its list of the most bike-friendly cities in the U.S. As I alluded to earlier in the book, Portland has regained its status as America's most bike-friendly city. Now we have our sights set on Amsterdam and Copenhagen. Of the churches which responded to the survey, it would be helpful for you to know that as a whole they represent the top-tiered bike-friendly cities from *Bicycling* magazine's list. In other words, the numbers will be reflective of this reality ... good or bad. So if churches in these top-echelon cities are knocking it out of the park in terms of being bikeable, bike-friendly, and bike-oriented and are strong in this regard then we can assume they're leading the *peloton*. However, if they are not reflective of the overall bike status of their city then we can also assume that possibly other cities don't have a chance. With that said, let's dig into the findings!

I received completed email surveys back from twelve churches that represented five cities and two countries (the U.S. and Canada). Ten out of twelve churches are currently in urban contexts. Two in particular are in their city's Central Business District (downtown) while the rest are mostly first-ring inner-city urban neighborhoods. To say it another way, most of the churches are in large urban contexts that are much greater or "thicker" in terms of density. These locales tend to be more bike-friendly and bike-oriented. Portland certainly is a bike-friendly city, but the further away from the downtown core one gets the lower the density and the less prevalent the bike lanes and bike boulevards. As with most "alternative" transportation, whether light-rail, streetcar, or bike boulevards, density in the both the built environment and the population is key.

My goal here is not to break down the responses to the survey from each and every church, unless you're tired and need something to make you sleepy. I do have a detailed list in the Appendix. But in general terms, here's how the results look:

Worship Attendance

How many people meet weekly at your church for the "main gathering?" In total, there were 5,305 worshippers among all 12 churches. The size of the churches surveyed ranged from 40 to 2,000, so I feel it was a good representation.

Bike Commuter for Worship

How many of that group commute to your worship gathering via bicycles? This is where things got interesting. Remember my 97 to 98 percent prediction? Well, I was almost right on. As a whole, the survey revealed that 69 to 92 people biked for worship which was about 1.3 to 1.7 percent of worshippers. The number did bump up in the months of nicer weather when 149 to 192 people commuted to worship gatherings on a bike. That percentage is at 2.8 to 3.6 percent. But even during these months of pleasant weather, 96 to 97 percent of worshippers still drove their cars.

There was some discrepancy in the numbers, because some of the churches build their church life around smaller neighborhood groups, gospel communities, or missional communities. Two churches in particular indicated that while Sunday gatherings showed a low percentage of believers who bike to worship, in fact upwards of 60 to 70 percent of people who make up these smaller groups actually do walk or bike since they are more geographic-oriented and based on proximity. They articulate the fact that the life of their church is lived out in these communities and Sundays are times when these groups all join together from all over the city. Many of these smaller gospel/missional communities can be quite spread out from one another. That is a good insight worth noting.

Does the Church Promote Biking? Do They Have Bike Parking?

Does your church promote/encourage bicycle transportation to your gatherings/events/church life? How? (That is, how are you promoting it or not? Do you have bike parking?) Most churches seemed to indicate that they do at least have bike parking whether they promote it or not. To be fair, when was the last time someone at a church gathering communicated a need for street-level car parking? It is simply assumed. But with bicycles, it is still imperative to keep promoting it. Two of the churches indicated that they had no bike parking at all. Those that did have parking only had enough for very a small number of riders. However, one church in particular did bring out additional bicycle parking for the warmer months. Still, there was no clear indication that any of the churches proactively promoted nor encouraged bicycling to the worship gatherings.

Miscellaneous

Anything else you want to add? One of the subtle themes that I picked up from the survey, which again was not remotely exhaustive, but merely representational, was the whole issue of families. That brings up the question ... do bikeable churches strictly appeal to young single urban hipsters? In other words, if someone has a family, does that make the matter of bicycling to a worship gathering neither doable nor desirable? I contend "no" and "no." In my neighborhood in inner NE Portland it is quite a common to see families out cycling together, especially on school days. If children and families can cycle Monday through Friday then why not on Sundays?

Recently my sons' school, Sabin Elementary, was featured in *Bicycling* magazine, along with Kona World and Bike Portland, for their national record-breaking numbers of bicycle commuters in their school bike train. There were 102 cyclists participating in the bike train. Two of my sons are longboarders, so they longboard to school instead of bike. The school won the first-ever "National Bike Train Competition."[4] On top of that, there is a conscious effort to educate children about the importance and joy of bicycling for exercise and transportation. Just last night, I was out on a bike ride with Seth, my youngest, and he was telling me all that he learned in school this past week about bicycling from hand motions for turning, riding on streets, pre-trip bike checks, safety, and so much more. This was an actual school program. Because it is part of the schools here, we're on the front end of seeing a

---

[4] http://www.biketrainpdx.org/national-bike-train-competition.

whole generation continue to downplay the car in favor of alternative modes of transportation. The question is, will the church follow suit or simply resist because of partisan political agendas? Or will we truly be missiologists and missionaries in our own cities?

Interpreting the Data

How do we interpret the data from the surveys? What does it communicate? What does it *not* communicate? Is the church in step with culture in terms of transportation issues, or are we stuck in a time warp where we're still favoring the auto? This indeed becomes challenging depending on the city you live in. Across North America, Portland is held up as the template for retrofitting a city for the bicycle, and many other cities are taking notes and learning from this city. From Dallas to Tucson to New York to Montreal, cities are more and more embracing the bicycle, not simply as a piece of recreational equipment, but as a viable transportation alternative. In Chapter 8, I will specifically give lots of ideas about creating a bikeable church. But first, let us take a step back and look at some underlying values, assumptions, and concepts about what it means to be a missionary and a missiologist to our cities.

Chapter 5

The Intersection of Missiology and Transportation Design

"For the first time since the car became the dominant form of American transportation after World War II, there is now a grassroots movement to seize at least a part of the street back from the motorists. A growing number of Americans, mounted on their bicycles like some new kind of urban cowboy, are mixing it up with swift, two-ton motor vehicles as they create a new society on the streets. They're finding physical fitness, low-cost transportation, environmental purity – and, still all too often, Wild West risks of sudden death or injury. These new pioneers are beginning to change the look and feel of many cities, suburbs, and small towns."[1]

In the same way that all Christians are, to some degree, theologians, we're all missiologists. We're theologians in the sense that we pour over Scripture daily in our love of, and devotion to, following the living God. The more we spend time with God, read the Word, and allow Him to transform us,

---

[1] Mapes, *Pedaling Revolution*, 7-8.

the more we learn about who He is. In a nutshell, that is theologizing. Although it conjures up images of heady intellectualism, dusty old books, dead authors, plaid jackets, pipes, and academia, theology is simply the "study of God." Mind you, study doesn't have to be mundane and academic; it can also be passionate and emotional, as in the way we "study" the people and things we love ... our spouses, children, sports, hobbies, food, hiking trails, coffee, music, and so on.

Missiology is "the study of missions." Like theology (missiology is a subset of Theology Proper ... just click on Wikipedia, trust me), missiology can be a rote academic exercise in mental gymnastics or a daily, real-life, flesh-and-blood, passionate pursuit as we point humanity to the reconciling and redeeming God. In a literal sense, every follower of Jesus is a theologian, missiologist, and missionary. God, the great missionary-God has called us out, redeemed us, transferred us from darkness to light, and then in turn sends us out to be His ambassadors of reconciliation between humanity and God. "Jesus said to them again, 'Peace be with you. As the Father has sent me, even so I am sending you.'"[2] If you haven't heard this yet, then let me be the first to say, "Welcome to the mission field."

Yes, you heard me correctly, you're a missionary. You probably chafe under that label and realization, but it is a reality you and I need to embrace. The problem is that most of

---

2 John 20:21.

us have narrowed the definition and parameters of what we think a missionary was or is. The images we conjure up in our minds, depending on if you grew up in the church or not, are white Europeans or Americans, with machete in hand, hacking through a dense jungle forest to get to a remote village in order to tell people about Jesus. Or maybe you think of young dudes in starchy white dress shirts going door-to-door to hand out booklets and tell you about God. But in fact, being a missionary means (1) you don't need to own a machete, (2) you don't need to wear starchy white dress shirts, (3) you certainly don't need to go door-to-door, and (4) you can simply be yourself where you're at. Can you swing it?

The apostle Paul, writing to the church in Colossae, explains, "Walk in wisdom toward outsiders, making the best use of the time. Let your speech always be gracious, seasoned with salt, so that you may know how you ought to answer each person."[3] Now there's a no-brainer. Paul's saying that even a super-introvert like me can do that. You see, we've let our imaginations run rampant, turning missionaries into super-humans with mutant abilities like the Avengers, X-Men, or Justice League, when the reality is they are no different from you and me. They are just like us and we're just like them. We *are* missionaries. Geography is not the defining factor of missions or what makes a missionary a missionary. We send missionaries to Africa, but Africa sends missionaries to

---

[3] Colossians 4:5-6.

America. We all need to be God's ambassadors of redemption and reconciliation.

The part that gets muddled is what missionaries work at. Being a missionary is a vocation (i.e., a calling) that is to be lived out in and through our occupation. Are you an urban planner? You're a missionary. Are you a bike mechanic? You're a missionary. Are you a barista? You're a missionary. You get the point. Now, I don't want to be dismissive of God specifically calling out people for certain tasks and roles whether at home or in a foreign nation. I'm all for that, but we need to come to the realization that wherever we go we're both missiologists and missionaries.

One of the roles of missiologists is to simply study the host culture of where they are living or where they are planning to live. To use an example, let's say we know of a young couple leaving the U.S. to become missionaries in another setting, context, and nation. Let's say their destination is Montréal, Québec. (That's in Canada, my fellow Americans.) We know that much of their training and preparation would be to study and learn not only the history of Montréal, but the larger story of Québec, Canada, and even France. (Montréal's roots are in France.) Along with that would be other key imperatives such as language acquisition. (They speak French there.) Once the couple arrives in Montréal, they'd learn to navigate the urban environment, including public transit and even the Bixi bike-share program (I had to throw that one in), nuances in local architecture as well as food delicacies and signature dishes like poutine, French fries smothered in gravy. In many ways, they're to become so well-versed in the culture and context of their new home that they begin to blend in and become an "insider."

As missionaries and missiologists here in our own setting and context, we should do the same, and try to study our own host cultures and cities with a fresh new set of lenses. I'm convinced that if we actually did do that, we'd change much of what we do as the church. Why? Because we'd look at our cities with the lens and perspective of an outsider coming in. Instead, we become lazy and simply assume too much, apply "imported" templates and models, and do and be church like they do everywhere else in Atlanta, Nashville, Omaha, Chicago, Orange County, or Cleveland. We'd cringe if someone exported these same templates to plant churches in Dubai, Mumbai, Berlin, Paris, Shanghai, or Moscow. We'd almost become irked and offended. We'd chide these missionaries for not planting contextualized churches and for being lazy missiologists. So why do we simply discard these same missiological principles here in our own setting? It is as if we're communicating that we have found the "right way" to do and be church, and that we simply need to export this model and plug it in here. The problem is that the culture has shifted and continues to morph, especially in places like urban Portland.

In my previous book, *The Multi-Nucleated Church,* I began kicking the tires of what a different missiological approach to cities could look like as I explored walkable (and even bikeable) churches. The goal is not to be creative nor innovative, but to simply study cities and let the built environment, culture, and transportation options influence the way we do and be the church and church planting. "To summarize, I am advocating that: (1) urban form dictates the how of church planting (while being guided by NT principles), (2) a new approach to church planting in multi-nucleated cities needs to develop around transportation technologies, (3) church planting networks in these settings can be both 'dense' and 'dispersed' as they are rooted in city centers but interconnected with other churches in the other city centers, and (4) the foundation of community in the church life of a city center needs to be pedestrian-oriented or walkable (and bike-friendly) which makes it accessible for those who live in such places."[4]

This is exactly where missiology and transportation design meet. On Friday mornings every other week, I have coffee with two urban transportation architects and designers. Their lives revolve around designing light-rail transit stations, bike-share stations, bike lanes, and so on. The conversations we have are fascinating and stimulating as we enjoy a good cup of Coava coffee in SE Portland. It is precisely this intersection of missiology and transportation that we talk about and explore. Two seemingly different and unrelated

---

[4] Benesh, *The Multi-Nucleated Church*, Chapter 1.

topics are brought together. There's the realization that they are really not that foreign to one another. In fact, they go hand-in-hand. You see, as missiologists, we know that transportation plays a pivotal role in how we do and be the church. Again, here comes the need for an extreme example to prove a point.

How would you plant a church in Mumbai or Shanghai where a large segment of the people get around on bicycles? Or let's say you're on the Mongolian Steppes and the horse is the only MoDo (mode of transportation)? Or closer to home, what about Manhattan where most travel is by public transportation (i.e., the subway). How would we do church and engage in church planting in each of these settings? It is pretty obvious that something seemingly simple, yet underrated, like transportation options, really becomes *the* primary (or one of the) influential factors for determining how a church is gathered and the daily rhythms of church life. Any attempt to force upon these cities an auto-oriented way of church would be like making Brazilian loin-cloth-wearing jungle tribes learn American hymns (in English) via pipe organ with a preacher in a three-piece suit. To do so would be to disregard basic missiological principles. But what about the bike?

"The idea is not to be novel or new, but as a missiologist to learn how to adapt around urban form. Simply put, we need to stop creating churches in our minds that are void of culture and context. It is the context of the city which is influential. Churches, while seeking to engage culture often overlook the transportation technologies that also play a major shaping role in cities."[5] I'm far from being a purist when it comes to bicycle transportation. I'm not advocating for some utopian society where we all wear homemade hemp clothing, sleep in VW Westfalia camper vans, and catch salmon out of the stream with our bare hands. All I'm asking is ... what if we planted churches with the bike in mind?

---

[5] Ibid., Chapter 3.

Chapter 6

Why Grown Men Shave Their Legs

"Hi, my name is Sean. I'm 38 years old, and I shave my legs."

I don't normally introduce myself like that, but I have. A few years ago, I was invited to speak to a university campus ministry in place of their campus pastor.

The leaders didn't seem to know anything about me. When it came time for me to speak, one of them got up and simply stated, "Well, we have a guest speaker tonight. His name is Sean." She quickly sat down. That was it ... crickets. I slowly made my way to the front as everyone stared at me, wondering who this dude was, what is he going to speak about, and why should we bother listening to him. I reached the front, turned around, leaned onto the music stand, and plainly stated, "You don't know me. You really don't know anything about me. What if I told you that I was 35 years old, unemployed, I live in my Mom's basement, I ride a scooter, and I shave my legs?" They all chuckled and giggled. Then I dryly said, "Everything I just told you is true ..." More crickets and a few gasps.

Indeed, it was all true. I was 35 then (check). Technically, I was unemployed as I was in between my previous job/ministry and my new one as a church planter in Vancouver, British Columbia (check). In our transition to Canada, we stayed for a while at my Mom's house. She has a big home in the country and we had the entire large basement to ourselves (check). I had (and still do ride) a scooter from time to time (check). I did this morning over to Ristretto Roasters. And I shave my legs (check). I told them about my days as a hiking and mountain biking guide and being out on the trail with such people as Oprah, Susan Sarandon, Ben Stiller, *Sports Illustrated* swimsuit models, Isaiah Thomas, and many others. Again, all true. It ended up being a fun evening with those college students.

I've been shaving my legs for about nine years now. When I began my work as a guide, while I was a church planter in Tucson, I was out on desert singletrack trails on a daily basis. If you know anything about the Sonoran Desert, you know that in the desert things either bite you, sting you, poke you, or poison you. Plants, animals, and insects alike have joined forces to punish humanity for venturing too close, whether we're talking about rattlesnakes, Gila monsters, prickly pear, cholla, black widows, saguaros, scorpions, and so on. In particular, when you're mountain biking on these trails, it means you're zipping past all of these potential threats at high speeds with rocks and cacti crowding in. That also means an occasional encounter with one or more of them.

On one of our mountain biking excursions, a good-looking middle-aged dude from England came out on a ride with us. He was stud-like, buff, and ripped. I'll call him "Pecks" for this story. Since destination spas attract more women than men, he had found a great fishing pond. Our group of bikers for the ride that day consisted of him and about six other middle-aged females. Since it was summer, even though we road early in the morning, Pecks thought it would be a brilliant idea to ride shirtless. Who could not resist a glistening muscled man mountain biking through the desert with the early morning sun peering over the Santiago Ridge casting his torso in a golden hue? The ladies followed him like a group of hens following a rooster in a barnyard.

But Pecks wasn't a good mountain biker. Since it was an easy-level mountain bike ride, we didn't venture onto nasty or gnarly technical trails. While we rode cactus-hugging singletrack trails, it was a relatively flat and rolling trail. On that day, I was the tail guide, and so I didn't get a close-up view on what transpired. Pecks was up front (of course) riding right on the tail of the lead (female) guide. When we came to a fork in the trail, she went left. Pecks didn't go left *or* right. He went straight. But there wasn't a trail there. In a last-minute effort to save himself, Pecks gripped both sets of brakes like he was holding on for dear life. The good news is, the bike stopped. The bad news? Pecks became a human projectile.

He landed, head-over-heels, smack dab into a large patch of prickly pear cactus. Shirtless and buff, Pecks was literally covered with hundreds of cactus spines. The thing about prickly pears is that they have both large spines, which are painful, but they are also covered with hundreds of small hair-like ones. These are small and as fine as hair, but painful and irritating. With tweezers in hand, the other guide and I spent the next half hour-plus picking cactus spines out of Pecks as he shook from the pain. We got most of them out, at least enough for him to ride back to the resort.

I remember well the first time I ran into prickly pear. It was late June and it was hotter than blazes. Another guide and I decided to take a run down a famous local trail called the Chutes after leading hikes and bike rides all morning. By the time we reached the top before our maddening descent, we were exhausted and on the verge of heat stroke. As a result, our motor skills were suspect. We hit a technical section, and I was floundering around and not focused. In the process of riding past a patch of prickly pear in a narrow chute, I tipped over into it. My whole right leg was covered with hundreds of these nasty hair-like cactus spines.

I stopped and attempted to pluck them out. The problem was that for every cactus spine I plucked out, I also grabbed a good two to three leg hairs. Ouch! After five minutes, I gave up, biked back to the resort, and headed home. It was on the drive home, with my leg full of cactus spines, that I decided to shave both my legs. (It would've been awkward if I only shaved one.) I had never done anything so cavalier before. I didn't tell Katie, nor did I really have any idea what to do. All

I know was that I grabbed her Venus razor and start hacking away.

I didn't even bother plucking out those cactus spines; I just shaved away. Now, I'm not a Sasquatch, but it was more involved than I had imagined. I felt like an adventurer or explorer in a pith helmet hacking my way through a jungle with a machete. I dulled the blade rather quickly, but kept on going. I didn't know I needed to take a pair of clippers first to my legs and *then* use a razor. After about an hour, I was done ... a bald Sasquatch. Chewbacca without leg hair. It was a funny sight to behold, all pink and bald. Over the next several days, I learned first-hand about the effects of razor burn, as I had these red welts all over. Nonetheless, I was clean-shaven.

Nine years later, I still shave. Not too long ago, Grant, our oldest son, asked me, "Dad, why do you still shave your legs? I mean, we don't live in the desert anymore." So I started growing my leg hairs out for about a month before I realized I couldn't stand it and shaved my legs again. I guess I'm a lifer. Sometimes people ask me how far up my legs I shave. My response? "All of the way to my neck." Well, not entirely true, but that opens up a conversation as to how far up does one need to shave. I've seen guys with what looks like "Chewbacca-shorts," if you know what I mean. Also, do you shave your feet? For a while I didn't, but then realized that I looked like a hobbit, so I started shaving those as well. (Sorry, Frodo.)

I've come to the conclusion that shaving my legs has missiological implications. Not only that, it is incarnational. Now before you think I am simply justifying what I do after the fact, hear me out. (Well, there might be a touch of justification.) Incarnation is when Jesus "took on flesh and blood" as He entered humanity. Humanity was added to His deity. He became like one of us. Not only was He tempted (but didn't sin), He also experienced the highs and lows of our emotions and physical limitations. He wept, was hungry, marveled, got fatigued, and so on.

Jesus also entered a very time-specific culture. He didn't enter humanity through the womb of a teenager as an *acultural* being. On the contrary, He was rooted in the culture of a first-century Jew: He followed Jewish customs, the Torah, and even Rome's occupation laws, such as paying taxes. On a deeper level, He experienced as well our pain, our suffering, as well as our joys and vibrancy. What a Savior we have! *He identified with us.* That is the concept of the Incarnation.

When we model Jesus' Incarnation, we identify with and relate to the larger culture around us, as well as the distinct cultural tribes that we personally identify with. In his book, *Bike Tribes: A Field Guide to North American Cyclists*, Mike Magnuson does a phenomenal job of identifying the various "tribes" within the bicycling community. Cyclists are simply not the same; in fact, there's a wide variety of them. The book is like a field guide for bicyclists. Magnuson observes:

70

Nevertheless, for very human reasons, because we don't want to be alone, cyclists tend to gravitate toward other cyclists with whom they feel the highest degree of "alikeness." People who race mountain bikes hang out with other people who race mountain bikes. People who ride bikes for fun hang out with people who ride for fun. It's a matter of group self-selection. Once cyclists become comfortable in their groups, they identify with these groups to the point where they occasionally think things like *This is the way we do it. That means this is the only way to do it.* Once cyclists think things like that, it becomes harder for them to appreciate that they are part of a larger community consisting of millions of people who ride bikes; instead, they are part of a smaller community consisting of a specific type of cyclist.

Most cyclists typically spend their entire cycling lives functioning within these small units: road riders or mountain bikers or fixie riders or triathletes or cyclocross racers or track racers or people who load their Chihuahua in a basket on a beach cruiser and ride off in the direction of sunshine and music and groovy people who don't want to sweat life's details.

Each of these groups has its own culture and history and a set of rules and normative behaviors. Let's call these groups Bike Tribes. Each of us is part of one tribal group. Each of us is curious about the other Bike Tribes, too, because in that one special way, because we love having two wheels under us, we're all the same.[1]

The more I immerse myself into the Portland bicycling culture, the more obvious this concept of *Bike Tribes* becomes. It just happens that Portland is home to a large variety of the bicycling species. In the same way the Santa Rita Mountains, south of Tucson, are home to a large variety of North

---

[1] Magnuson, *Bike Tribes*, Chapter 1.

American birds, including exotic species from Central America, Portland is a bicyclist's paradise for North American cyclists. But which tribe to I affiliate with?

This has taken me a while to figure it out and I am still in process. While I ride a singlespeed bike, I'm not one and the same as a young hipster on a fixie singlespeed. Plus I don't look good in skinny jeans. Even though I ride a lot on the road, I am not a roadie. I have a strong aversion towards spandex. I wear baggie mountain bike clothing while riding my singlespeed bike on the road. I don't ride a tall bike. I don't carry a small animal on my bike in a basket. I don't pull a trailer with music blasting out of it. I have rain gear, but I am not your typical neon-glow-in-the-dark bicycle commuter.

So which tribe do I lock in with, and how do I incarnate the Gospel among them? These are questions that missionaries ask. I am a missionary. You're a missionary. Maybe God has called us to reach *tribes* that we relate with, or maybe God wants us to reach *other* tribes. The *other* could mean for me to hang out with (gulp) spandex-wearing roadies. It could also mean a tribe in another part of the city (or world) where we don't share the same ethnicity or mother tongue. With that in mind, I keep shaving my legs, because it is a simply act of Incarnation, not to mention that I still enjoy it. Well, not the shaving part.

Chapter 7

Reengagement

During the course of writing this book, something surprisingly fun and refreshing happened. Much of my experience in bicycling has been in mountain biking, in particular being a mountain biking guide taking hundreds and even thousands of people out into the desert for fun and adventure. I did this while I was a church planter and a church planting strategist in Tucson. I left that industry and way of living when we moved away from Tucson about four years ago. Since then I've had a lot of time to reminisce on those five years that I was a guide. They were some of the best experiences of my life and even some of my most authentic on-the-fly ministry experiences, just being a listening ear to people whose lives or hearts were broken.

Since then, my tires have not seen a whole lot of dirt, to be quite honest. Relocation plus schooling and writing projects kept me busier than I would've liked to admit. On top of that, juggling church planting, campus ministry, starting urthTREK, seminary teaching, and a family was and is a creative act. In fact, my mountain bike spends most of its days just looking at me in my living room. It is probably wondering why we don't hang out much anymore and even jealous of my urban singlespeed bike that I ride daily for commuting, errands, and exercise. I still ride lots, but almost exclusively on the road.

Since arriving in Portland, I've been looking for something to do on the side in the bicycling community in order to reengage. Since Portland is a bicycling mecca, I knew that my limited bike mechanic skills would be suspect when it comes to qualified and skilled mechanics. I kicked around getting certified and trained as a bike mechanic through schooling at the United Bicycle Institute. That's still an option. I have no sales experience, so working in a bike shop is out. I've applied for a number of bike-related non-profit jobs, but to no avail. I had an interview to deliver soup via bicycle and that didn't work out. Finally, I received a call, then an interview, and then a job offer, and then a job. I took it.

I am now once again a cycling guide-cum-church planter. I'm just not the knobby-tire off-road mountain biking kind like I used to be. But this suits me just fine and I've thoroughly enjoyed jumping into helping people experience the city of Portland and surrounding areas all by bike, whether it's riding through the Pearl District downtown, being mesmerized by the many cascading waterfalls of the Columbia Gorge, a jaunt through wine country, or a ride up the Oregon coast. It is all epic. I get the privilege of informing and educating people about why Portland is deserving of its platinum-level status of being a bike-friendly city.

Another added benefit is that I join the throng of daily bicycle commuters into Portland's downtown core. Whereas before I'd commute a few times a week to several of my local coffee shops for writing, prepping for teaching, meetings, and so forth, now I make a beeline to downtown and in the process cross one of the many bridges (Burnside) that span the Willamette River. It is of utter importance to wear waterproof gear. It is already the first week of June and yesterday my commute was in 50-degree rain-soaked weather. Our Columbia Gorge tour, with its high winds, fog, and rain, felt more like a mid-February tour than a summer tour. It was epic nonetheless.

In fact, a key ingredient of Portland's bicycle culture is your ability to be waterproof. There's nothing more miserable than showing up for a meeting in wet jeans. If you're lucky, you can find a bathroom with a high-powered hand drier and contort your body just the right way to dry off your jeans. Yes, you too remember that episode from the Mr. Bean movie when he did the same ...

Cycling has now been etched into Portland's storyline. You cannot separate Portland from it, just as you can't separate Portland from its micro-brewery scene, its rain, its hipster enclaves, or its weirdness. Portland is now defined by the bicycle more than by any other mode of transportation. I am grateful and stoked to be a part of it. That is one of the primary reasons behind the writing of this book, since so many people I know don't even own cars but instead bike everywhere. When we lived in Vancouver, BC, it made sense to talk about church planting in terms of mass transit, including the bus, Skytrain, and Seabus that link the various city centers dotted throughout the metro area. In Portland, it makes sense, missiologically-speaking, to talk about church planting with the bicycle in mind. The rest of the city is thinking about the bike for transporting goods and services from coffee (Trailhead Coffee[1]) to beer (Old Town[2]).

With that said I've slowly begun working my way out onto the trail. When I look at my mountain bike in my living room it at least smiles because we're taking more excursions off road. While Portland is truly a cycling mecca, the reality is that the off-road kind of biking is rather suspect and seriously lacking. You'd think that being surrounded my mountains and volcanos that mountain biking plus Portland's outdoor vibe would equal epic trails. Not so. In fact, to get to the good trails means loading up your bike and *driving* an hour to an hour and a half to the trailheads.

I've found urban cycling to be a great connection point with those we'd deem "far from God" whether through alternative lifestyles or simply an alternative cultural viewpoint or framework. Last night we went to some friends' house for a BBQ. Walking up to their front door, their front gate is plastered with anti-religion placards, anti-Christian

---

[1] http://www.trailheadcoffeeroasters.com.

[2] http://www.oldtownpizza.com.

door-to-door notes, and other mostly anti-Christian stuff. However, we lifted the latch and walked on through. Most of the conversation that evening revolved around urban cycling in Portland and since I'm now an "expert" as a cycling guide they peppered me with questions about new places to ride and so forth. Again, the common denominator was and is the bike.

But how exactly should we embark on church planting with the bicycle in mind? The next chapter is a do-it-yourself guide to planting bikeable churches and making established churches more bike-friendly.

Chapter 8

The DIY Bikeable Church

If there were any city that has fully embraced the DIY (Do It Yourself) mentality, it is Portland. In his book, *Brew to Bikes*, local Portland State University professor Charles Heying (and a group of Masters and PhD urban planning students) set out to explore, research, and figure out Portland's rapidly budding artisan economy. What they realized, and what the book revealed, is that there's something in the city that breeds entrepreneurs. Not entrepreneurs in the sense of big business start-ups, sports cars, and a lot of flash and hype. Rather, these are people who simply just start doing, creating, networking and building, with little to no resources.

As I've already mentioned, oftentimes I start my morning out at Ristretto Roasters on North Williams. The building that houses Ristretto (called the HUB) is also home to many other artisan start-up companies. The common storyline is that many of these types of businesses simply started as a dream, an idea, a passion, and a conviction. Not only that, but they started simple and small ... at the kitchen table, roasting coffee with an 80s popcorn popper (Ristretto), in the basement making longboards the low-tech way (Subsonic[1]), or welding together bike frames in a home garage (Pereira[2]). No big overhead and often little or no start-up costs. They pieced together what they had, networked widely and learned from others, and simply began experimenting, tweaking and fine-tuning. The rest, as they say, is history. Could we start bikeable churches in the same manner?

The answer is a resounding "YES!!!" Why not? What do we have to lose? No hype, no big splash, little or no upfront or start-up costs, but simply a dream, a conviction, and a passion is all it takes. The bikeable church is definitively DIY to the core. Here's my honest and humble admission: I've never seen nor heard of a bikeable church, a bike-friendly church, nor a bike-oriented or bike-focused church. That doesn't mean they don't exist or that there are not churches making attempts or leaning in that direction. I've heard from several people already about their church, or ones they know, attempting to take a stab at making their churches more bike-friendly and accessible. Some of the programs initiated are "bike to church" days or adding bike parking during the more pleasant months of the year. I affirm those attempts and am encouraged.

Colby Henley of Tucson, who's a friend, church planter, bicycling enthusiast, cycling writer/blogger, and an advocate

---

[1] http://subsonicskateboards.com.

[2] http://www.pereiracycles.com.

of bikeable churches, recently wrote an intriguing article for *Tucson Velo* called "Bicycles and Faith: Combining transportation and religion." Ironically, Colby quotes me in his article from my book *View From the Urban Loft*, but that's not why I am bringing his article up. (That'd be a bit awkward and self-serving.) He brings up some great points and makes some key observations about the role of bicycling and gathering for worship, as he looks at religion broadly for the sake of the article and audience. He asks some penetrating questions that should be reflected on, such as "If you practice a faith, do you think the distance/method you travel to worship makes a difference? Would you be more inclined to attend a service that accommodated bicyclists or was within biking distance?"[3]

Thus we're paving the way for bikeable churches. I want to be upfront and admit that what I'm suggesting is in the realm of concepts or steps that I myself am attempting to make. That is my full disclosure. This is also the line of differentiation between various kinds of books. First, there's the book written by the successful practitioner. We've all read them whether related to church start-ups that became large and influential, business start-ups that became global icons, and so forth. These authors carry a lot of weight because they're taking you on the journey of how they went from rags to riches (and how you can too, if you follow their principles). Next is the strategist-writer. They have their pulse on the

---

[3] Henley, "Bicycles and faith."

culture, or whatever line of work they're in, from high-tech to church planting to music, who forecast and tell you where the trends are heading. We watch them on talk shows, listen to their lectures as they forecast the future of transportation or biomedical research, and we devour their books. They are strategic thinkers who are backed up by great research and possess the intuition to apply it. Lastly, there's the theoretician. This is the person who lives in the world of ideas, what-ifs, and possibilities. They're the ones who come up with bizarre theories or futuristic design concepts for bicycles, cars, or housing. You'll hear them talk about creating fully enclosed offshore mega-cities that are self-sustaining. You watch them on Nova, PBS, the Discovery Channel, or National Geographic.

The Bikeable Church is a synthesis between the strategist and the theoretician. Honestly, that's the way I'm wired. Also, since I'm on the front end of conceptualizing what bikeable churches can and could possibly look like, I'm wrestling with how to actually do this myself. Maybe I'm being too honest, but that is who I am and where I'm at. One of my hopes with this book, as well as my others, is to stimulate the conversation as well as stretch our thinking when it comes to various church- and church planting-related topics. In *Metrospiritual,* I looked at the geography of church planting and began conceptualizing what church planting in gentrifying neighborhoods could look like. In *View From the Urban Loft,* I advocated for the need to develop a robust theology of the city in order to be about holistic community transformation. In *The Multi-Nucleated Church,* I sought to create a template for church planting in high-density polycentric cities. Which brings us up to *The Bikeable Church*.

For the remainder of this chapter, I will set forth concepts and ideas about how we can go about starting bikeable, bike-friendly, and bike-oriented churches. This comes from personal reflection, observing the bike scene in Portland, as well as rubbing shoulders with professors, architects, designers, and those who earn their livelihood from the bike industry. As church planting "tribalizes," we're seeing a continued uptick of churches that cater to specific demographics. We have cowboy churches, country-western churches, biker churches (the Harley-Davidson kind), recovery churches, prison churches, and so forth. It is time to include bikeable churches in the mix. The question now becomes ... how? Let me share with you some ways to start a DIY bikeable church. This discussion will be blended in that there are action steps of creating a bikeable church from scratch as well as suggestions of how to make current churches more bike-oriented.

The first step would be to simply begin by *educating people about the joys and benefits of bicycling*. While this may seem like an overly simplistic and unassuming step, it is crucial and foundational. It was amazing to read the story of Mia Birk, Portland's former bicycle coordinator, who helped push forward the cycling revolution in Portland. She started simple by meeting with dozens of groups from the Lion's Club to business owners and so forth. She knew that in order to move the city in the direction of being more bike-friendly she needed to personally share her story, talk to the masses, and get people on board. It worked. Whether you're an established church, a new church plant, or on the front end of developing your church planting strategy, it'd be beneficial to do likewise. Cast the vision. Talk about the benefits of being a bikeable church, whether it be for health, lowering carbon emissions, or creating a more sustainable city. Kingdom work is about redeeming both urban people and urban places.

My second suggestion, and these are not necessarily in order of importance, nor in a step-by-step manner, is to *add or ensure ample bike parking*. The survey revealed that among those churches that actually did have bike parking, it was either downplayed, not mentioned, or so insignificant or minuscule in size that it communicated (subtly) to worshippers that if you want to hang with us you better drive. One church in particular has 1,200 worshippers on a given Sunday, but bike parking for only ten or fewer bikes. And yet this church is very much in a higher density urban neighborhood at the intersection of a vast network of bike routes throughout the city. One can easily bike there from all over the city, as it is centrally located and *very* accessible. What if that same church added a bike corral on the street out front and gave up one to two parking spaces? If the medium is the message, then a bike corral would communicate lots, not only to the church but to the neighborhood and city.

Some churches can easily add sheltered parking, well-lit parking, or even indoor parking. If your neighborhood is crime-prone, you'll need to ensure that someone won't have to worry about their new *Eighthinch* fixie bike won't get jacked. Along with this, a church could offer bike locks and have them on hand in case people forgot theirs. When I eat at the Hopworks Bikebar I always notice a wall of numerous bike locks they carry in case you forgot yours. Epic idea.

Do bike-related activities as a church. This could range from a bike-in movie night, bike-to-zoo day, or heck, a bike-to-church day. Here in Portland, there is a phenomenon known as Sunday Parkways that happens in each quadrant of the city. What happens is a traffic loop is blocked off to all cars, so that people can get out and bike without worrying about auto traffic. This past weekend, Sunday Parkways was in my part of the city; it attracted over 20,000 riders. Various local companies and food carts were out en masse offering the cyclists everything from burritos to bicycle maintenance. What if a church scrapped or rescheduled its regular Sunday activities and biked or helped out? The ideas of bike-related activities that a church can host or participate in could fill a whole book in and of itself.

Become a bike advocate for your neighborhood. What if you or your church advocated for more bikeable or "complete streets"?[4] This is the concept that roads are to be for everyone ... cars, bicycles, buses, and pedestrians. How could your church partner with the city planning department or your local neighborhood association to help your streets become safer for all those who use them and who need to use them?

Provide bike maps to your gatherings. Whether you're handing out physical maps on Sundays or having downloadable pdfs on your church website, this would be helpful, and be one more way the church could communicate a great deal about how you not only value alternative transportation, but also healthy lives and sustainable cities. Other ideas would be to have links on your website to Google maps where people can enter in their home address and then get directions to where the church gathers via the bicycle routes through the city. Once people arrive at your gathering, you could also make sure they know where to park their bikes.

Safety clinics for kids and families. In the same way that schools here are proactively educating students about bicycle safety and transportation, what if the churches did likewise? Since it's more than likely you don't live in inner-city Portland, you and your church could start something yourself. Not only that, but you could partner with the local schools in your area, talk to some local bike shops, and bring onboard your city's bicycle coordinator or transportation planner. This could go a long way towards building goodwill and being a

---

[4] http://www.completestreets.org.

blessing to your city. Teach kids how to bike on streets and in bike lanes, proper riding protocol and etiquette, safety, and bike handling. Instill confidence in them as well as how to bike in their city neighborhoods. Once the kids buy in, soon you'll have more parents becoming more interested as well.

Support a bike salvage/repair co-op. There are non-profit groups in each city (or so it seems) that fix or repair bikes for their lower-income and marginalized residents. This is a worthy organization to partner with, volunteer with, bless, and support. Oftentimes they are seeking to partner with and work with schools in lower-income neighborhoods through education, teaching bicycle maintenance skills, and getting more kids on bicycles for health. Why not join in their efforts?

Install showers and make them available to your people. This may not seem very doable, but it is worth a shot. One of the reasons people hesitate bicycling to a worship gathering is they arrive dripping with sweat. If you're in the South or Midwest in the summer, it can be stiflingly muggy. If you're in the Southwest, it can be oven-temperature hot. Many people don't want to hassle with sweat, especially if they're going to be in a room (big or small) with 40 to 2,000 other worshippers for an hour and a half. So why not have showers on site? There are so many businesses here locally that have showers for this very purpose, along with secured indoor parking, to encourage more bike commuting. Why can't the church do the same?

It will take modeling by the leadership. Yes, we're to be imitators of Christ, and no, I'm not asking you to be imitators of Lance Armstrong. It doesn't matter if you have a bad tan line and your calf muscles are, well, undefined, because there's no stronger message than setting an example. If you bike to meetings with people in your church, and especially to Sunday gatherings (even with your whole family), that will communicate a lot. Church leaders should always consciously convey to others through their actions and lifestyle that they are modeling Christ, and so be able to say, as Paul did, "Imitate me as I imitate Christ." They model tithing, discipleship, parenting, how to treat the barista, how much to tip, and so forth. This is why as a cyclist I don't blow through stop signs, even when there are no other cars around, because how can I in turn tell my boys to obey the rules of the road if I don't?

I had a good reminder of that six months ago. I was on a lunch time bike ride. It was right before Christmas and in pouring rain. Traffic was light and I was passed by another cyclist. That got my competitive juices flowing, especially since he was only wearing jeans. I kicked into a higher gear (figuratively speaking, since I ride a singlespeed) and began tailing him. We came up to a stop sign, and I watched in horror as he blew right through it. How dare he?! So ... I followed suit and blew through it myself. I felt pretty smug, as I was thirty feet behind him. I then noticed flashing lights. I looked over my shoulder and my heart sank. I was being pulled over by a motorcycle cop. Doh! Of all the times I decided to blow through a stop sign! Bad timing.

He walked up and I profusely apologized, admitting I knew it was wrong. He said, "Listen, I live in this neighborhood with my family. The last thing I want to see happen is for you to run a stop sign and for my wife to hit you in our minivan with the kids inside." Ouch, point well taken. He then told me that the fine was like $260, but since it was right before Christmas, he was going to be "giving and gracious" and let me off with a warning. I was relieved and humbled. As soon as I got home, I told Katie and the boys what happened. We laughed and they chided me, because I was always telling them not to blow stop signs. Point taken. I need to be always modeling road safety to them and to others. No exceptions, no excuses.

More bike-related event ideas. There is no end to bike-related events that a church can put on and host. Bike polo for your hipster crowd, a coffee or pub crawl on bikes, or family bike rides. At our local Hopworks Bikebar you can sit out front and pedal a bike that helps generate electricity for them to brew beer with. What fun to see something like that at a church gathering? Generating all your electricity – PowerPoint, lights, computers, sound system, etc. – with pedal-power? Far-fetched? No, not really, since it is already happening in our cities.

Appoint a bike coordinator. This could be a volunteer or a staff position. This person would spearhead your church's efforts to be bike-friendly, bike-oriented, and bikeable. Let the pastors do what they're called to – prayer, leading, teaching, etc. – but have someone else take the mantle of leading the church to become more in sync with the larger changing trends in the city in regards to transportation. Again, you may think this is far-fetched, but think of this as you and me brainstorming together.

Liaise with the city. Related to the last idea, what if your church had someone (the bike coordinator would be a good fit) who worked with the city (planners, engineers, politicians, etc), local bicycle groups and organizations (non-profits, advocacy groups, etc), bicycle businesses (bike shops and touring services), and bike-powered businesses (pedal powered delivery services). This person would be your bike culture networker who bridges the gap between the church and all of these various other groups, businesses, and entities. The conversation and the story is already taking place in our cities, but will we as churches step in and become part of the dialogue?

These are a few ideas of some easy and practical steps that you can take to make your church more bikeable, bike-friendly, and bike-oriented. Remember, the focus or backbone of this conversation is missiological in nature. To ignore that foundational principle would simply make these attempts novel, quaint and cute. There's nothing wrong with doing these things in and of themselves. I'm also not trying to say that everything we do has to have twelve Bible verses and a doctrinal position paper to back up each one. Instead, I want to take this moment to again remind you that you are both a missionary and missiologist. I'm simply trying to stimulate our thinking in that direction.

.

Chapter 9

Simplicity

I'm a mountain biker trapped in the body of a singlespeed urban cyclist. I tell people that I feel most alive when I'm on some great singletrack trail zipping through the mountains. There's something holy, spiritual, sacred, fulfilling, and downright fun about mountain biking. The longer I'm an urban cyclist, the more I feel many of those same sensations while riding the streets of Portland. It's an addiction, except that the side effect is a healthy lifestyle. It is a sport and hobby of risk. If you're not getting hurt out on the trail you're probably not pushing yourself enough. Once in a while that can translate to the streets as well. Since I don't like pain, I usually ride to the upper limit of my comfort threshold and just kind of stay there. I have a family to take care of, for crying out loud! I don't think Katie and the boys would enjoy feeding me jello and wiping my chin for the rest of their lives, if I got seriously injured. Nonetheless, I still ride, and take risks.

As much as I try to avoid pain and mayhem on the trails, you can't be in the biking community without encountering them. I love my scars, shaved legs, and tattoo, because they're an instant connect within the culture. I was at a coffee shop talking with a friend who's an avid road cyclist and mountain biker, when this other dude was walking by on the way to the john. His arm was in a sling and he was walking with one crutch. As he passed by me, he saw my shaved legs and mountain bike tattoo above my right ankle. Instant connect. He stopped, talked, and told his story. It's interesting how within the biking world you're instant friends. He went on to tell us of his recent run-in with a Lexus SUV coming down the road. Despite a few broken ribs, knee surgery, and a broken collarbone, he was all smiles as he told his story. Afterwards, my friend and I began lifting up sleeves or pant legs showing our scars and telling our stories.

My favorite scar is from a mountain bike ride in the desert outside of Tucson. I was biking at the resort with a fellow guide and we were about a mile out. The last big obstacle to tackle was a twenty-foot-wide dry and sandy wash bed. The sand is thick, and you need all the momentum you can muster to make it across, only to have to climb up a sandy slope to get out of it. It's a fun challenge. I was almost through the wash when my right foot slipped out, shot forward, and hit my front tire. My leg then was thrown back and went right into my chain ring. Ah yes, and it was a brand new chain ring as sharp as a knife. (This was one of the reasons why I later switched to singlespeeds.) Luckily (sarcasm!) my left leg was peddling because when my right one hit the chain ring, it sliced me right open. I was filleted. I looked down and all I could see was the white skin and the fat in it down to the tendon. There was about a six-inch, perfectly sliced open gash on the back of my leg starting at my heel and working its way up. So I did what any other mountain biker would do ... I rode back to the shop, took photos, and then I went to the emergency room.

In our world, stories are big and we all have them. Stories are what define us a lot of times. However, personhood is something that is defined in the context of relationships. Who am I? I'm a husband, a father, a son, a sibling, a friend, and a child of God. I am defined by the relationships that I'm in. I like that kind of image. Who you are isn't really what you say you are as much as who you are in your relationship with others. How have we redefined our image today? We've turned our focus inward and elevated individualism.

We want sex, power, prestige, good looks, great intellect. And why? Because we all want to be loved. But since we mistakenly think our image comes from within, it then becomes all about making our names great. Why do some pastors want big churches? Let's be real honest. To be known. To be loved. To be approved. To be accepted. Bikeable churches are definitely moving in the opposite direction; small-scale, simple, and nondescript. Why do we want to make a lot of money? So we can buy cool stuff to impress people, so that they'll like us. Why do we want good looks or a good looking spouse? Because they make us look good. Why do we crave to be noticed? Because we want affection and approval. What would it be like if we had an outward focus instead of an inward one? What if relationships helped define us instead of success?

I love going home. I grew up in small-town Iowa. I really only get home once every two to three years, if that. It's funny how things don't really change in small towns. What once seemed like a thriving metropolis of a city now only takes five minutes to drive across. Once I left home to go to college, I realized how small it really was and is. I like that. Here's why I like to go back. Because when I go back people say, "Ah look, there's Sean, he's Gary and Janet's boy." There's something in that statement that resonates in my heart. It's a statement of identity not predicated on performance or achievements. It didn't matter that I was the quarterback of a 1-9 football team in high school. When I go home all I am is Sean. People like me for who I am. They have no idea who I've become, where I've gone, or even what I do. That kind of stuff doesn't really matter because I was loved and accepted before I could ever shoot a basket, or throw a football, or even get past kindergarten.

My soul is at rest in Tama, Iowa. I don't have to be pretentious or put on a show. They'd see right through it, anyways. It's hard to impress people when they remember you as a gangly junior higher with pimples and a squeaky voice. Yet we live in a culture that tries to define people by performance and a shallow definition of success. One of the reasons why I'm a proponent of bikeable churches is that it slows things way down and centers us on relationships. What if we instead received our identity of personhood from relationships? More importantly, what if our image came from our relationship with God? You see, there's no impressing God. He's kind of like the people in my hometown who love and accept me simply for who I am, but even more so. God loves and accepts us for who we are as His children. I think it's funny for us to try to get pretentious with God, but we do. We try and impress Him with our devotion and zeal. But I think oftentimes God simply remembers when we were new believers fumbling our way around the Bible and our new faith.

I'm really trying to work on my image. I've had a pretty skewed view for years. The grip of performance is lessening its hold on me. It's slow and painful, but healthy. I'm healing, I'm growing, and my view of who I am is changing. I've learned to be okay with obscurity. I've learned to be okay with being normal and dealing with normal struggles. I once thought that I would change the world and everyone would see that I'm some really spiritual guru. And now? I'm broken. I'm a leaky vessel with cracks. However, I'm still God's vessel of redemption and reconciliation. If He ever wants to do something with me, then that's His call. I'm growing content to love God and love everyone I meet. To linger in a coffee shop and listen as people share the junk in their lives. To show approval when people reveal the deep struggles of their soul. To love freely with no strings attached. I'm tired of trying to impress. I'm lousy at it. Regardless of what happens in this life I'll always and proudly be Gary and Janet's son. Most importantly, I'm God's child. When I get these things right, I can love Katie, Grant, Camden, and Seth unselfishly. Who I am is who God made me, and has nothing to do with what the world thinks of me. I'll take my chances with what the King of the Universe thinks.

There's something refreshingly simply when I think about bikeable churches. When you ride, you're caught up in the rhythms of the city, you're intimately connected with the weather, and you simply notice a lot more. While at times you may be bombing down a hill faster than the speed limit (I didn't say that) you mostly notice people. You are well aware of the other cyclists around you, pedestrians on the sidewalk, and in regards to cars, you're seeing people in them more than the machines. It's all rather simple. That probably explains my rationale for riding singlespeed bikes. I don't have to fret or worry about my derailleur being out of whack nor the need to keep up with the components arms race. I hop on and ride. Simple.

What if church could be that way? What if the story of my discovery of the bike shop in the Introduction were normative for the way a church gathers? No hype, no hoopla, no pretentiousness, but instead relationally-driven. I know, I know ... I can already hear and feel the pushback. "But Sean, the Great Commission *demands* that our churches be large." Maybe not every local expression has it in its DNA to be mega-anything other than mega-awesome at who they are and who they're trying to reach. As a parent, my goal is not to have really large children. That'd be kind of odd when you think about it. Instead, I want them to be lean, healthy, and of course, to "multiply" when they're happily married adults.

In church planting, bigger isn't better, it's just bigger. Better is better. Not every church has in its DNA to be an elephant or a blue whale. Most are like rabbits or hamsters. Trust me, if you've had the latter as pets you know the reproductive potential. I'm not here to cry foul at the large church; nor am I here to solely advocate for the small church. Just be yourself. With that said, if we're honest as we talk about bikeable churches, then it may preclude certainly a smaller gathering. But who knows? Maybe fifty years down the road, if Portland surpasses Amsterdam, we might be able to see bikeable churches grow rather large. Let's push for multiplication rather than largeness as our defining factor for success. Some may grow large and we'll rejoice, but the goal is to keep multiplying.

When we advocate for simplicity, we hone in on relationships with people whose stories become essential. There was this cycling guide … let's call him Will. He ended up meeting a Victoria's Secret manager at the resort I worked at, they fell in love, and he moved to another city with her. He and I'd talk for hours when we'd do training excursions. He's a sharp guy who listens to NPR a lot. At one point he became an evangelist for the church I was starting (he's not a follower of Jesus). We'd sit at lunch and he'd try and get people to come to my church. Sometimes he'd see someone, lean over the table at me, and say, "Sean, we gotta get her in your church. She could really use God and a good support network." I liked that. I told him I'd give him ten percent of any person's tithe if he got them into our church. He was on a mission.

Another time we did a three-hour training outing together. We must've covered every controversial subject under heaven; homosexuality, gun control, free trade, education, politics, abortion, pre-marital sex, and God. Those canned five-minute Gospel presentations don't do justice. We must've talked about God, Jesus, the Gospel, and salvation for at least an hour of that conversation. He'd ask such deep questions. I have never talked to anyone about the Gospel in such detail in my life. It was awesome. Here's the best part. That night he called his Victoria's Secret girlfriend (this was before he moved) and told her all about our conversation. The next morning, he came up to me. "Man, Sean, dude, I was on the phone with" … let's call her Sarah ... "last night and I told her everything we talked about." At this point he was ecstatic. Here's what he told me that he told her, "Sarah, you should've heard me and Sean's conversation today. We talked about gays, guns, and God. It was awesome! Man, we talked a lot about God!" When was the last time we shared the Gospel and it was such good news that the recipient was that pumped? Did Will come to Christ?

No. Did I fail, because he didn't turn his life over to Christ? No, because that's not my job. I'm simply the messenger.

Simple bikeable churches are relationship-driven. The beauty of the bicycle is that it causes us to slow down enough to become more in touch with ourselves, our bodies, people around us, the local environment, and the setting and context of our cities. More so than with driving, we're fully present in the here and now rather than sitting in bumper-to-bumper traffic listening to the radio to pass the time. My point and intention in this book is not the make cars out to be evil (as I said, I have one and use it), but to call us back to a more simple, simplistic, and slower way of church planting and church life. Maybe something seemingly simply like a bicycle is just the right tool for that ...

Simple. Just the other day, as I was reading in the Psalms, I came across Psalm 116:6, "The Lord preserves the simple; when I was brought low, he saved me." I'm not going to attempt to jump into word studies about the deeper meaning and the linguistic development of the word "simple" and its field of meaning. That word simply jolted me that morning and I was reminded on 2 Corinthians 11:3, "But I am afraid that, as the serpent deceived Eve by his craftiness, your minds will be led astray from the simplicity and purity of devotion to Christ" (NASB). Simple. Following Christ should be about our simplicity of love and devotion. In a similar way, I am convinced church planting should be about the same ... simplicity.

We've distorted both following Christ and church planting into being about techniques, methods, structures, forms, functions, templates, and so forth. Isn't it time that following Christ and likewise church planting returned to this kind of simplicity? Maybe it is the bicycle that will get us there ...

Appendix

Bikeable Church Survey

Survey Sampling

	Location	Size	# of People Who Bike	Bike Parking?	Are You Promoting Bike Parking?	Other Notes
Church #1	Urban	1,200	20 (1.6%)	Yes, but space for less than 10 bikes	No	Lots of families
Church #2	Urban	2,000	10-20 during winter months, 80-100 during summer months (.5-1% winter, 4-5% summer)	Yes, and additional bike parking is brought out during the summer months	Yes	The church does not do anything actively to promote people bicycling to church at this time
Church #3	Urban	115	0	No	No	
Church #4	Urban	600	10-12 (1.6-2%)	Did not say	Did not say	Church meets in hilly downtown and has many families
Church #5	Suburban	260	1 occasional youth (.5%)	No	No	Located on a road with no bike lanes

	Location	Size	# of People Who Bike	Bike Parking?	Are You Promoting Bike Parking?	Other Notes
Church #6	Urban	200	5 (2.5%)	Yes, bike parking in secure / visible location	Yes	Located on a neighbor-hood street in area of town with high bike ridership
Church #7	Urban	150	4 (2.6%)	Plenty	No	
Church #8	Urban	120	5-10 (4-8%)	Yes, but space for less than 10 bikes	No	60%-70% of gospel com-munities members bike or walk to gatherings
Church #9	Urban	200	5-9 (2.5-4.5%)	Did not say	No	We have a small but committed group of bikers but do not promote it widely
Church #10	Urban	40	5 (12.5%)	Yes	No	Lots of families
Church #11	Urban	100	2-4 (2-4%)	Yes	No	There may be more people coming by bike who don't park in our worship space that I'm not aware of
Church #12	Suburban	320	2 (.006%)	Did not say	No	The pastor bike commutes a few times a week
TOTALS		5,305	69-92 (1.3-1.7%) 149-192 *Summer* (2.8-3.6%)			

Bibliography

Benesh, Sean, *The Multi-Nucleated Church: Towards a Theoretical Framework for Church Planting in High-Density Cities* (Portland: Urban Loft, 2012), Kindle edition.

Birk, Mia, *Joyride: Pedaling Toward a Healthier Planet* (Portland: Cadence, 2010).

Henley, Colby, "Bicycles and faith: combining transportation and religion," *Tucson Velo,* March 29, 2012, accessed May 25, 2012, http://tucsonvelo.com/blog/bicycles-and-faith-combining-transportation-and-religion/12258.

Heying, Charles, *Brew to Bikes: Portland's Artisan Economy* (Portland: Ooligan, 2010).

International Making Cities Livable, "Why Aren't Young People Buying Cars? *International Making Cities Livable,* accessed June 16, 2012, http://livablecities.org/blog/why-arent-young-people-buying-cars.

Lassa, Todd, "Why Young People Are Driving Less," *Motor Trend,* August 2012, accessed June 20, 2012, http://www.motortrend.com/features/auto_news/2012/1208_why_young_people_are_driving_less.

McCracken, Brett, *Hipster Christianity: When Church and Cool Collide* (Grand Rapids: Baker, 2010).

Maus, Jeff, "Woman dies in collision with 18-wheeler on SW Madison," *BikePortland,* May 16, 2012, accessed June 2, 2012, http://bikeportland.org/2012/05/16/collision-at-sw-3rd-and-madison-leaves-woman-with-life-threatening-injuries-71838.

Magnuson, Mike, *Bike Tribes: A Field Guide to North American Cyclists* (Emmaus: Rodale, 2012).

Mapes, Jeff, *Pedaling Revolution: How Cyclists Are Changing American Cities* (Corvallis: Oregon State University Press, 2009).

Murphy-Gill, Meghan, "Have you ever ridden a bike to church?" *U.S Catholic*, June 13, 2012, accessed June 15, 2012, http://www.uscatholic.org/blog/2012/06/have-you-ever-ridden-bike-church.

Newman et al, *Resilient Cities: Responding to Peak Oil and Climate Change* (Washington, DC: Island, 2009).

Streeter, April, *Women on Wheels: A Handbook and How-To for City Cyclists* (Portland: A Serious Press, 2012).

UN-HABITAT, *Global Report on Human Settlement 2009: Planning Sustainable Cities* (London: Earthscan, 2010).

Other Books by Urban Loft Publishers

They're Just Not That Into You: The Church's Struggle for Relevancy in the 21st Century (2012) by Stephen R. Harper.

Close to 90% of Canadians say they still believe in God, yet fewer than 15% go to church on a regular basis. Why is there such a disconnect between church and culture? *They're Just Not That Into You: The Church's Search for Relevancy in the 21st Century* explores this question. Author Stephen Harper delves into the curious shift that has occurred in western society, studying the cultural nuances affecting the church's ability to significantly influence the world around it. So is there a solution? *They're Just Not That Into You* investigates this reality and offers some practical solutions.

"Through rich theological reflection, sociological evaluation, scientific survey and sharing the stories of rooted Christian communities, Stephen Harper offers the Canadian - and global - church a valuable resource for engaging and adapting our faith practices for the advance of the missio dei in our post-modern, pluralistic realities. We need churches which are willing to release their agendas in submission to the work Jesus desires to do in the lives of the individuals and communities we have been called. Harper's work and experience offers a framework through which to do just that."

-- Jon Huckins is on staff with NieuCommunities, is the Co-Founder of The Global Immersion Project & author of *Thin Places* & *Teaching Through the Art of Storytelling*

The Multi-Nucleated Church: Towards a Theoretical Framework for Understanding the City (2012) by Sean Benesh.

For too long, church planting literature and training have been primarily focused on starting churches in low-density parts of our cities predicated upon auto-based commuting patterns. However, the reality of the global city is that millions upon millions of people worldwide do not live that kind of lifestyle. Rather, life revolves around getting from Point A to Point B via foot, bicycle, or public transportation. What would church planting then look like with those common transportation realities? Instead of basing strategies and methodologies on a car-based lifestyle, *The Multi-Nucleated Church* reduces the scale to walkable neighborhoods, districts, city centers, and central cities. The common denominator is truly high-density urban contexts. *The Multi-Nucleated Church* explores the theoretical framework of constructing an ecclesiology that finds its home in the multi-nucleated high-density mega-global city.

"Sean Benesh is a practitioner who is also doing theological work – and in the fastest growing, most complex human environments in our world. Moreover, he loves the city and understands the nuance of place. His analysis contributes to a more effective and incarnational engagement for the church. Thanks, Sean!"

-- Dr. Len Hjalmarson, Adjunct Professor of Ministry at Northern Baptist Theological Seminary, Chicago and co-author of *Missional Spirituality* (IVP: 2011) and *The Missional Church Fieldbook* (Lulu.com).

About the Author

Sean Benesh (DMin, Bakke Graduate University) lives in the Pacific Northwest and is involved in urban ministry in the capacity of professor, researcher, consultant, director of the Epoch Center for Urban Renewal, and church planter. He blogs regularly on various urban themes and topics at theurbanloft.org. Sean is married to his high school sweetheart, Katie, and they have three sons who are passionate longboarders, Grant, Camden, and Seth. Sean is a mountain biker and an urban cyclist. He has experience as a mountain biking, hiking, and urban cycling guide in Arizona and Oregon. In 2009, Sean started urthTREK, an outdoor adventure non-profit that that has as its mission to "connect urban with wilderness."

About Urban Loft Publishers

Urban Loft Publishers focuses on ideas, topics, themes, and conversations about all-things *urban*. The city is the central theme and focus of the materials we publish. Given our world's rapid urbanization and dense globalization comes the need to continue to hammer out a theology of the city, as well as the impetus to adapt and model urban ministry to the changing twenty-first century city. It is our intention to continue to mix together urban ministry, theology, urban planning, architecture, transportation planning, and the social sciences as we push the conversation forward about *renewing the city*. While we lean heavily in favor of scholarly and academic works, we also explore the fun and lighter side of cities as well. Welcome to the *new* urban world.

www.theurbanloft.org
Portland, Oregon

Made in the USA
San Bernardino, CA
19 September 2014